SIGNPOSTS FOR LIVING

A PSYCHOLOGICAL MANUAL FOR BEING

DR KIRSTEN HUNTER

BOOK 1
**CONTROL YOUR CONSCIOUSNESS –
IN THE DRIVER'S SEAT**

BOOK 2
UNDERSTANDING MYSELF – BE AN EXPERT

BOOK 3
**MINDFULNESS AND STATE OF FLOW –
LIVING WITH PURPOSE AND PASSION**

BOOK 4
**UNDERSTANDING OTHERS –
LOVED ONES TO TRICKY ONES**

BOOK 5
PARENTING – LOVE, PRIDE, APPRENTICESHIP

BOOK 6
NAILING BEING AN ADULT – HAVE THE SKILLS

A MEANINGFUL LIFE

DEVOTE YOURSELF TO:

1. **KNOWING** YOURSELF,

2. **LOVING** OTHERS,

3. **LOVING** YOUR COMMUNITY,

4. **GRATITUDE** FOR THE MOMENT, AND

5. **CREATING SOMETHING** THAT GIVES YOU MEANING AND PURPOSE.

First published 2021 by Kirsten Hunter

Produced by Indie Experts P/L, Australasia
indieexperts.com.au

Copyright © Kirsten Hunter 2021

The moral right of the author to be identified as the author of this work has been asserted.

Except for the purposes of reviewing, no part of this publication may be reproduced or transmitted in any form or by any means, electronic or mechanical, including photocopying, recording or any information storage or retrieval system, without the written permission of the author. Infringers of copyright render themselves viable for prosecution.

Cover design and image by Zach Lawry @ Mates Rates Screen Printing & Design
Edited by Jane Smith @ www.janesmitheditor.com
Internal design by Indie Experts
Typeset in URW DIN by Post Pre-press Group, Brisbane

ISBN 978-1-922742-00-1 (paperback)
ISBN 978-1-922742-01-8 (epub)

Disclaimer: Any information in the book is purely the opinion of the author based on personal experience and should not be taken as business or legal advice. All material is provided for educational purposes only. We recommend to always seek the advice of a qualified professional before making any decision regarding personal and business needs.

To Jon

PREFACE TO THE SERIES

This series of books is actually a conversation that I have had with thousands of people over the last twenty years of clinical psychology work. From approximately 42,000 hours of conversations with clients of all shapes and sizes and from all walks of life, all struggling during their various stages in life, I have learnt so much. When you have the same conversation that many times and you see progress, you see where the value lies. I want to share this conversation with you.

'Signpost for Living' is written out of sheer frustration and exhilaration in equal measure. I have limited hours with my clients. This series of books is the information, across the breadth of 'being human' areas, that I would cover with clients if there was no limit to time. This is my 'ideal situation' series, to share with others how to understand and master ourselves. We are pretty dodgy at being human. We really have very little clue about how we work – we don't fully understand our emotions, our behaviour, our neurology, our physiology – or how to live with purpose, calmness, contentment and joy, with our loved ones and within ourselves. This series covers all of these life-challenge hotspots and things we need to learn about ourselves. If we get support, encouragement, and general guidance in these areas, we can get on track quickly. Life can expand and boom us into more contentment and happiness.

How amazing life is if we allow it to be.

If you get a new puppy, it is wise to put in the time to train it; you can enjoy your pup so much more once it's trained. Your pup becomes easy and fun to walk, reliable on your carpets, and an enjoyable character. This is strangely true for *us* too. By studying our thinking, emotions, behaviour and styles of relating to others – really getting a solid level of self-awareness and having a robust skillset – we can enjoy ourselves and our world so much more. And no, we do *not* need to be puppies to learn new tricks; we can learn as adults, at any stage of life. No excuses here. It is absolutely, profoundly, exasperatingly ridiculous that we do not all learn this information routinely at school. 'How to be human, class 101'. Humans have the code to develop physically, but we need more information to develop psychologically into full adults. Not learning these basic life skills can leave us feeling insecure, disconnected and unsafe.

Life is growth. Life is a work in progress.

This is what these books are about. We do not know everything about 'being human' – far from it – but we do know a fair bit. This knowledge, which comes largely through the profession of psychology, is not, however, common knowledge. And yet it should be. It needs to be. We need a manual for being human, for without it we are driving blind.

This series is based on clinical evidence and sound reasoning. It provides clear, calm direction – not all the answers, but solid signposts. Time to share this knowledge with everyone.

WHAT TO EXPECT IN THE 'SIGNPOSTS FOR LIVING' SERIES

The books in the 'Signposts for Living' series are independent but complementary; by strengthening and cultivating one area you enhance all of the other areas simultaneously. There is not much point fixing one hole in the boat when the other holes are not receiving attention. This is not a piecemeal series. We need to cover the whole of human functioning. In this series there will be chapters you need, chapters you don't, chapters that talk to you now, chapters that will tap you on the shoulder in your future. The 'Signposts for Living' series is written for everyone: all ages, mums and dads, grandparents, young adults and teenagers finding their way.

The books are broken down to first explore (in Book 1) how controlling your consciousness can help you grab the reins to your nervous system, thoughts and emotions. Relevant side-alleys that are common traps to dodgy thinking are included. We then flesh out your personal issues in Book 2: *Understanding Myself*. The importance of being awake in life and aware of your present moment is celebrated in Book 3, along with the gem of living with purpose and passion in a state of flow. 'Signposts for Living' then broadens in Book 4 to discuss understanding our relationships with our people (the good, the bad and the ugly). The true complexity of parenting is then dissected in Book 5. Finally, the art of nailing being an adult is fleshed out in Book 6, revealing the excitement of reaping the rewards of becoming a thriving mature human.

To make the books as concise and user-friendly as possible, I have avoided references, footnotes and other scholarly tools as much as possible. The goal is for you to be able to access and use this valuable information without feeling bogged down or needing to have specialised, background knowledge. To acknowledge my sources and guide you to delve deeper, if you wish to, I have included 'further reading' lists where relevant at the end of each book.

Welcome to understanding your humanness.

BOOK 1
CONTROL YOUR CONSCIOUSNESS – IN THE DRIVER'S SEAT

CONTENTS

CHAPTER 1	HAPPINESS: AN EXTRAORDINARY LIFE	1
CHAPTER 2	YOU EITHER EXPAND OR CONTRACT	5
CHAPTER 3	CONTROLLING YOUR CONSCIOUSNESS	6
CHAPTER 4	MINDFUL SELF-INQUIRY	10
CHAPTER 5	MONKEY MIND	13
CHAPTER 6	BRAIN SURGERY WITHOUT ANAESTHESIA	16
CHAPTER 7	MINDFULNESS IS THE ANTIDOTE	17
CHAPTER 8	STUDY ALL OF YOUR MOMENTS	22
CHAPTER 9	COLLECTIVE CONSCIOUSNESS	23
CHAPTER 10	YOUR NEW NORMAL	24
CHAPTER 11	WHY DO WE BOTHER WITH ALL THE DISTRACTIONS?	25
CHAPTER 12	NEGATIVE THINKING: CONFINED BY OUR OWN MINDS	31
CHAPTER 13	PSYCHOLOGICAL ARCHAEOLOGY: 'YOUR ISSUES'	34
CHAPTER 14	NATURE … NURTURE	37
CHAPTER 15	STORM AND SUNSHINE: PESSIMISM VS OPTIMISM	38
CHAPTER 16	'NOT ENOUGH', 'ONE DAY', 'NOT BAD' MANTRAS	45
CHAPTER 17	FEEL A BIT BROKEN: INTRO TO DEPRESSION AND ANXIETY	47
CHAPTER 18	ANXIETY: 'WHAT IF, WHAT IF, WHAT IF …'	53
CHAPTER 19	DEPRESSION	70
CHAPTER 20	LIVING ON AUTOPILOT	74
CHAPTER 21	THE 'SHOULDS': DRAGGING YOURSELF THROUGH LIFE	76

CHAPTER 22	TRAIN THE MIND	78
CHAPTER 23	RIVER OF CONSCIOUSNESS	82
CHAPTER 24	CHOOSE TO DANCE OR 'PASS': YOUR THOUGHTS	84
CHAPTER 25	HOW JUDGEMENTAL ARE WE!	91
CHAPTER 26	DON'T BELIEVE EVERYTHING YOU THINK: IRRATIONAL BELIEFS	92
CHAPTER 27	YOUR NEGATIVE SELF-TALK IS YOUR INFORMANT	94
CHAPTER 28	EXTREME NEGATIVE SELF-TALK	96
CHAPTER 29	LEVELS OF CONSCIOUSNESS	98
CHAPTER 30	YOUR DYSFUNCTIONAL STYLES OF THINKING	101
CHAPTER 31	FIGHT THE GOOD FIGHT; ARGUE WITH YOURSELF	106
CHAPTER 32	OUR EMOTIONAL LAG	112
CHAPTER 33	EMOTIONAL WILDERNESS	117
CHAPTER 34	EMOTIONS WASHING OVER YOU	119
CHAPTER 35	WISDOM: THE COMMITMENT OF INTELLIGENCE, EMOTION AND WILL	124
CHAPTER 36	PANIC: FIGHT / FLIGHT / FREEZE / FAINT	126
CHAPTER 37	OUR AUTONOMIC NERVOUS SYSTEM	138
CHAPTER 38	MIND-BODY CONNECTION	141
CHAPTER 39	FORMAL MINDFULNESS PRACTICE	143
CHAPTER 40	NEUROPLASTICITY	168
CHAPTER 41	SELF-HYPNOSIS	170
IN CONCLUSION	KNOW THYSELF	171

FURTHER READING	172
ACKNOWLEDGEMENTS	173
ABOUT THE AUTHOR	175

CHAPTER 1
HAPPINESS: AN EXTRAORDINARY LIFE

Happiness in not a state that we can demand. We cannot decide to 'be happy'; it is a by-product of doing life well, with meaning. It's not a matter of 'I'm going to *be* happy today'; it is 'I'm going to *achieve* happy'.

A state of contentment and happiness comes from learning, growing, building, creating and loving. So many people sit idle, complaining that they are not happy. Why would we be happy if we are not building our lives? If we are simply treading water? Happiness is not an endpoint. If we expect to just be happy, research has shown that we are more likely to be depressed, anxious and lonely.

A strange analogy ... if we want to warm our body temperature, we move our body – we exercise. We can't just sit there and say, 'I want my body to be warm, I want it to just happen spontaneously, I demand it.' Our *doing* creates the body warmth; that is *our* responsibility. So too with happiness: it is our doing, our living that creates our 'happy'. Clients come into my psychology practice saying,

'I'm not happy'. They do not like my response of, 'Well why would you be? You are not living. Let's start living.'

This idea that I *ought* to be happy – expressed like a demand – is a dangerous idea. It's as if we receive 'happy' from the universe rather than create our conditions to experience joy. This seems to be a contemporary disease in Western society: a sense that we're entitled to be happy and a fear of sadness. We actually become anxious because we have an expectation that we should just be happy, and if we are not, we feel as if we are missing out. Happiness has not been delivered to us on a platter. Happiness could equally be called 'wholeness'. We must create this wholeness.

> Happiness = wholeness.

The question of happiness can be traced back 2,300 years ago to Aristotle, who concluded that the individual is actually in charge of their own happiness. Abraham Lincoln agreed, famously saying, 'Most folks are about as happy as they make up their minds to be.' It is within most people's power, regardless of their circumstances, to *decide* to become happier, rather than living on autopilot. So many people walk around with a sense of meaninglessness. They seem half-asleep, even when they're busy doing things they think are important.

Rather than chasing dissolving distractions (like a busy daily fluster or a focus on image and status), the way you get meaning into your life is to devote yourself to loving others, your community around you, and to creating something that gives you purpose. As will be explained later on, it is not what is *happening* in our lives, but our *interpretation* of our life circumstances that leads to our happiness. We as individuals need to privately learn to control our inner experiences to determine the quality of our lives.

> Our *interpretation* of our life circumstances leads to our happiness.

We cannot directly reach for happiness; it is the beautiful by-product of a life lived well. Happy people lead vigorous lives, they are open to a variety of experiences, they keep on learning until the day they die, and they have strong ties and commitments to other people and to the environment in which they live. They find enjoyment in whatever they do, even if it is difficult or tedious; they are rarely bored, and they can work with anything that comes their way – they can take it in their stride. Undoubtedly, their degree of adaptability is their greatest strength. Happiness is the lovely side-effect of living well. It is living well that needs to be our focus and our responsibility, not happiness.

*I've realised how strong I have become.
I'm just not insecure anymore.*
Reggie, twenty-nine-year-old client

Being happy has extraordinary benefits. Happier people live longer and have fewer health problems. Positive emotions protect us and lessen the effects of aging; happier people have better health habits and immune systems, and lower blood pressure. Happier people are significantly more satisfied with their jobs, and have more productivity, higher income and more gainful employment. Happier people endure pain better.

The sensory system of happy people expects a 'win:win' encounter, rather than anticipating a fear response. As a result, when faced with a life challenge or problem to solve, they can activate their capacity to be tolerant, to be expansive and creative in their mindset. Their positive feelings facilitate optimal functioning at interpersonal, intellectual and physical levels.

CHAPTER 2
YOU EITHER EXPAND OR CONTRACT

People who live well have a buoyancy to their presence. We can be either expanding or contracting. Expansion involves understanding, awareness, connectedness and love. Contraction involves ignorance, fear, avoidance and hatred. If we are not moving forward in life, we are moving backwards. To be healthy and resilient, life needs to expand. Open-mindedness is the key to expansion. If you do not expand your life, and you just stay with the familiar, you run the risk of deadening your spirit. The 'Signposts for Living' books involve simple truths about being a healthy human. The stakes are high; if you don't learn to live well, you risk losing the chance to have a life worth living. To be happy we must learn and grow. But how?

CHAPTER 3
CONTROLLING YOUR CONSCIOUSNESS

There is a simple truth that has been understood across the ages and across cultures, religions and philosophies: that the control of our consciousness determines the quality of our life. All of these philosophers and disciplines (Aristotle, Socrates, Stoicism, Christian Monastic Orders, Buddhism, Taoism, etc) seek to free our consciousness from the influence of outside biological and social forces. Learning to control our consciousness is equivalent to gaining a human superpower. If there is one skill worth mastering, this is it. Our reward is a more enjoyable, richer and more meaningful life, in which we are equipped to deal with obstacles and suffering.

How do you gain control over your thoughts and therefore, to a large degree, your emotions? How can you work towards ridding yourself of your anxieties and fears and become freer of the controls of societal pressures?

> *The mind is everything;*
> *what you think, you become.*
> Socrates, Greek philosopher

First thing first: how does consciousness work? Your consciousness results from a combination of the incredibly complex architecture of your nervous system and your choices. We have to work with and alongside our biological forces – in other words, our nervous system. You could think of your nervous system as a vehicle. You can get into the driver's seat and take some control of how you want to think, act and ultimately feel about your world.

Our consciousness is an extraordinary machine that takes internal and external information and processes it to create meaning and actions. Our consciousness sieves through our perceptions, ideas, feelings and sensations, and then prioritises this vast amount of information. Our brain functions in two ways; we have a primitive brain and a higher-order brain. As a result, we not only have reflexive and instinctive responses, but we have an ability to contemplate, to create, to analyse. This means we can imagine wonderful creations and theories – but we can also concoct irrational and false interpretations of events that cause us great fear when we believe them. We can use our consciousness to be cruel to ourselves.

Our consciousness sieves through our perceptions, ideas, feelings and sensations.

Regardless of what is actually happening in our outside worlds, we can make ourselves miserable rather than happy, purely by losing control of our consciousness. Two people may see exactly the same event, but one may transform a hopeless situation into challenges to overcome, while the other sees defeat and disaster. You can learn to control your consciousness so that you persevere despite setbacks and obstacles. This is an amazing skill that sets a person up to succeed and to enjoy more of life.

An absolute legend of a role model is Viktor Frankl, who demonstrated the sheer power of a healthy mind. Frankl wrote *Man's search for meaning* in just nine days, immediately after being released from a Holocaust concentration camp. Frankl demonstrated profound wisdom and control of his consciousness as he was able to maintain his mental health and compassion throughout this extraordinary trauma. He epitomises the power of the mind over situational stress. His experience emphasises what we are going to cover: the power of choosing to let emotions pass over you with calm recognition so that you are not avoiding or drowning in them.

Controlling your consciousness means controlling what happens in your thoughts from moment to moment. This involves mindful self-inquiry. We need to understand how consciousness works and how it is controlled – because only if we understand how we subjectively shape our world can we master this. Everything we experience is represented in the mind as information. If we are able to control this information, we can *decide* how we experience our lives.

We will first look at the mechanics of controlling our consciousness, and then we will focus on increasing our moment-to-moment choices and awareness.

CHAPTER 4
MINDFUL SELF-INQUIRY

There is nothing wrong with the mind; it is a good tool, but it makes mistakes a lot of the time. The mind can be reactive, petty, greedy, egotistical, short-sighted and inaccurate. It is only really our healthy mind that we want to celebrate and take the lead from, and this is a mind with awareness.

A quiet mind can give you serenity. You can gain mindful self-inquiry by experiencing and focusing on your own individual being. With this practice, you are watching your own self *being* yourself: your thoughts, your emotions, your bodily sensations and your behaviour, all of which can contribute to anxiety, stress and depressive mood. You are the observer and the observed. You could start to question: 'Am I the thought or the thinker? Where do I reside in myself?' And then this awareness of yourself becomes larger and larger and larger. And you become more and more conscious of everything: your thoughts, your emotions and your behaviours. Understanding yourself is the goal – working towards freedom from the restlessness in your being. This exploration, while extremely worthwhile, can be surprising, as fears often lie beneath the surface of our awareness.

This process is about becoming free to determine our own experience of the world. A large part involves becoming aware of which of our responses are socially conditioned. For example, we might recognise that we desire a product only because an ad is making it seem attractive, not because we really want it. We do not want to be a puppet to marketing; we do not want to be controlled from the outside. We want to become more independent of how our body responds and take charge of what happens in our mind.

> *Pleasure and pain occur in consciousness*
> *and exist only there.*
> *If you are pained by external things,*
> *it is not they that disturb you,*
> *but your own judgement of them.*
> *And it is in your power to wipe out that*
> *judgement now.*
>
> Marcus Aurelius, Roman emperor and philosopher

Since what we experience is our reality, we can transform our reality to the extent that we are aware of and shape what happens in our consciousness. It's not an *issue* that causes our fear but our *view* of an issue. This type of awareness is a process of 'checking in' with yourself. You can do this when you are facing a difficult time, or have a burning desire for something, or are tempted to put off something that is good for you. Or you can just take a quiet time to do a general check in with how you are going. Quiet times like driving or walking are good check-in times. You can use this time to ask yourself, 'How am I travelling? What's on track for me? What is not? What are my pressures? What are my priorities? How am I going with looking after my health?' This is a time for reflecting and being aware.

We need to *not* look around at others or at our outside environment. We need to look inward; this is what shapes our experience of ourselves, of others and of our worlds. We feel grounded from being connected with ourselves – from within, not from outside. You are not your car, your job, your status, your house; you are *you*. We will come back to this theme of living with a care, a compassion and a love of yourself.

Everything you need to know (and the ownership of it!) is right there under your nose. You already have all the information you need; you just need to open your eyes to your thoughts, feelings and behaviour – and take back the puppet strings.

CHAPTER 5
MONKEY MIND

Our left cerebral hemisphere is prone to major fabrications, faulty interpretations and misjudgement. The constant whirring of the brain, the constant cycling of thoughts is in Buddhism affectionately called 'monkey mind'. This is the distracting rattle, the 'buzzing' of our brain. 'What if this?', 'What if that?', 'Got to do this', 'Got to do that'. Our brains have some serious traffic. The average person has approximately 60,000 thoughts per day. The vast, vast majority of our thoughts are repeats from the day before, and the day before that. Same monkey show, different day. We will cover how to slow down this traffic, how to get the mechanics right. Not just so there is less traffic to navigate and make behave, but for pure peace of mind and increased tranquillity.

We have a culture of 24/7 connectivity. We also have a culture of doing more and doing it faster. Welcome to our modern world. This is just fuel for our monkey mind. The sheer volume of information that we are exposed to accelerates our pace of living, and everyday living seems to be getting more complex. In our mad rush of daily activities and demands, we are exposed to an onslaught of daily news with an out-of-proportion focus on trauma and gloom. When we lived in villages, we had only our community to be concerned about; now we have the world's affairs at our doorstep. While we should be aware and mindful of world events such as global warming, violation of human rights, economic crises, health epidemics and famine, the problem is that we have limited skills and capacity to deal with this in a helpful and healthy way. The fact is, our brains get overwhelmed by this pace of life and bombardment of information, leaving us susceptible to misjudgement, major fabrications, faulty interpretations, panic, anxiety, frustration, and self-judgement. The problem is our inability to manage our monkey mind, our racing fearful thoughts. We must cultivate our inner resources for dealing with this stress.

Our frenetic pace is not conducive to reflective thinking. It's too fast for us humans. We don't have time to proactively adjust, to work out our priorities, or to be effective and meaningful in what we're doing, when we are running around madly, continually reacting and being plugged in. While our new 'time-saving' technologies are meant to give us more down time, we have actually become even more switched on and in 'go' mode. Every timeframe gap is filled. Even waiting at bus stops. We don't leave work and enjoy the sound of the birds, the soft dusk sunlight, the trees and flowers around us. We check emails, check news and ensure that we are being fed some sort of stimulation or entertainment. We have even become fearful of sitting and *being* – of quiet moments, of taking in our surroundings.

Technology has freed us up, only to imprison us further. It's created the imperative to go faster, to take on more ideas, and to juggle more.

CHAPTER 6
BRAIN SURGERY WITHOUT ANAESTHESIA

You're about to closely observe your thoughts, your feelings and your behaviours. It could be ugly. You could be hearing one insult after another. This is why Tibetan meditation master Chogyam Trungpa said humorously that meditation was like having 'brain surgery without anesthesia'.

With mindful self-inquiry, you're looking into a mirror and you are naked with your thoughts, feelings and behaviour. Mindful self-inquiry is an honest conversation with yourself. You are face-to-face with your insecurities, prejudices, judgements, fear, shame, guilt and other familiar themes. This is the skill of learning to create a space between yourself and your thoughts, feelings and behaviours. Through mindful self-inquiry, you can decide how to manage them, reduce their power over you and shape them so that in the future they are not frequent visitors but float towards the distance. With time, you can learn to have more control and to acknowledge difficult thoughts and feelings, understand and respect their origins, and experience deeper states of acceptance and inner calm.

CHAPTER 7
MINDFULNESS IS THE ANTIDOTE

What is **mindfulness**? Mindfulness is simply observing, watching, examining your thoughts, your emotions, your body and your behaviour. The 'how to' of mindfulness is covered in Book 3, Part 1. Mindfulness is about being fully aware of what is happening within yourself and around yourself moment to moment.

Think about a time when you were really happy. I can bet that you were focused on the situation and truly absorbed, not thinking about a myriad of other distracting thoughts. You want more of those times in your life? Well, here's how.

Be present as your life unfolds *in this moment*. Slow down and appreciate, rather than rushing and looking for future 'better' moments. This is your life *now*. This is what counts. Your reactive mind can be like a washing machine. This is about getting out of the washing machine, and instead watching the contents of the washing machine from the outside. Watching the spinning of your mind.

Mindfulness consists of cultivating awareness of the mind and body and living in the here and now. While mindfulness as a practice is historically rooted in ancient Buddhist meditative discipline, it is a skill that we can all benefit from.

> Mindfulness is the verb.
> The action.
> The practice.
> Make it your lifestyle!

With this practice of moment-to-moment observation of the mind and body, you come to see life as a process of constant movement and change. You are able to monitor yourself with a curious mind and acknowledge all aspects of your experience. The goal is for us to work towards a calm and focused approach to this awareness, with less stress and more inner balance. Mindfulness is a powerful vehicle to help us understand our mind and body better, and to help us recognise the causes of our mental and emotional torment. The emphasis is on having the right *attitude* when watching our mind. This matters much more than focusing on *what* we are watching or feeling. How you relate to what is happening with your mind and your body makes a big difference to the degree and nature of the psychological and physical pain you feel.

We need to be patient with our own minds when practising mindfulness. It is about understanding the nature of our minds. We do judge a lot of the time, we do get tense and frightened, and we are not going to get immediate results. We therefore need to take our time with this.

Mindfulness can be extremely beneficial in regard to many different difficulties and disorders. It is only in the present moment that you can make changes, so it is this moment-to-moment awareness that you need to rely on to bring focus to your problem. Mindfulness allows you to see your experience clearly, allowing you to become more aware of how you are affected by stress. It teaches you to become aware of and monitor unconscious habitual tendencies. It is then within your ability to *choose your response*. This allows you to take an active role in your health and well-being and your moment-to-moment experience. You choose your actions with insight and clarity and with more ability to work towards desired outcomes.

With this information you are not a judge but a scientist; you are studying yourself. Rather than reacting to stress with unconscious habitual patterns, you can learn to respond to stress mindfully, choosing to respond more skillfully. There will always be disturbing experiences, thought processes and crises. Mindfulness teaches us to expect these complicated times, these emotional storms. We learn that in the scheme of our life, now is the time for a very hard chapter, but we get in and work with it and through it. We understand that ultimately, we will find meaning and purpose through these hard times. For now, however, we need to put our head down and work with ourselves. Old maladaptive coping techniques like substance abuse and workaholism that might be our reaction to stress can be replaced with new ways of transforming stress. We are moving from mindlessness to mindfulness in our response. Mindfulness allows you to bring clarity, awareness and an ability to tolerate a wide range of negative feelings like fear and agitation.

Mindfulness or mindlessness?

With a scientist's mindset you are working to understand your habitual ways of thinking. This has enormous potential to help you alleviate your stress and negative emotion. You might be surprised once you begin your mindfulness lifestyle. You might find that your mind tends to have two modes of thinking: either rehashing life events or rehearsing for the future. You may have already been aware of how busy your mind is. But do you realise how routinely you are not present for what is happening in this moment?

Think about how minor daily stresses affect your thoughts and emotions, and then as a result your body. You may feel stressed out when stuck in traffic, or when you are having an unpleasant conversation. You might also experience stress reactions just anticipating these events. You might feel headaches, muscular tension, stomach upset and sleep problems, or long-term effects like heart disease, cancer, alcohol abuse, overworking, and overeating. Mindfulness can have an enormous impact on all of these health issues and day-to-day stressors.

Formal or informal mindfulness practice grows practice by practice. We need to be patient when our mind is agitated. We need to be patient with our mind's ever-human tendency to wander. If we choose to focus on an activity in the present, we do not need to follow these wandering travels. We do not always need to be *doing*, or filling up our moments with activity. We can just *be*; we can just be present in absorbing our environment and in our interactions with people. Practising patience means being completely open to each moment, letting things unfold in their own time, accepting our current moment in its fullness.

CHAPTER 8
STUDY ALL OF YOUR MOMENTS

Your mistakes, your joy, your mind, other people, your passions, your failures, your successes, your work, your body, your interactions, your lifestyle, your pain, your attitudes – study *all* of your moments. Every moment reflects back to you information about your mind and your body. Trust the wisdom of your own direct experience.

CHAPTER 9
COLLECTIVE CONSCIOUSNESS

If we become skilled in our individual consciousness, we can begin to work towards changing the collective consciousness. How can we have a peaceful approach to others and the world's needs if we do not first have peace within ourselves? Mindfulness means practising taking responsibility for yourself and learning to listen to and trust your own being. If we learn to take more responsibility for ourselves, surely we will become better at taking responsibility on a broader scale – for our people, our neighbours, our planet.

CHAPTER 10
YOUR NEW NORMAL

To launch into an advanced new level of self-awareness and thrive, obviously you need a mind that is open to learning. You can't solve an old problem with the same mind, so you need to open your mind.

In practising mindfulness, you have to bring your whole being to the process. This requires a lifelong commitment to continual inquiry and refining your perspective as you acquire new levels of understanding of self and others. Just as you can't unlearn the skill of reading, you can't undo knowledge and self-awareness. And why would you? This level of functioning becomes your baseline, your new normal. You can't close your eyes to what you have seen.

CHAPTER 11
WHY DO WE BOTHER WITH ALL THE DISTRACTIONS?

Most of us have the illusion that life will be complete, and we will be happy when we are richer, thinner, more attractive, and more successful. We are surrounded by messages that we need to stay young and have a great (and conventionally attractive) body. Then we will live happily ever after. We believe when we see people who are rich, famous and good looking that they are living rewarding and contented lives. Perhaps this is why we enjoy hearing when they have fallen on hard times.

Our society worships materialism. We are like Augustus Gloop from *Charlie and the Chocolate Factory*, gorging ourselves on new toys, cars, technology, clothes, sparkly and trending things. And we are of course helped along by marketing – sorry, brainwashing – with ad upon ad telling us how we should look and what we 'need'. We are constantly being manipulated to consume. Brainwashing involves showing something over and over again and pulling on our emotional heart strings.

Can you imagine how many times per day you are exposed to advertising? Unless we are in nature, it is in our face everywhere we turn. We come to believe we must own things. Our goal is to have more and more money. More property equals success. More, more, more. We are in a high-spin cycle and we don't even know it. We have lost perspective on what is actually important.

We can become so consumed by the material world that we forget about what is really important: compassion, generosity and love. We will often forgo needs for wants. People are so hungry for life satisfaction that they look to meet their needs through consumerism. But we can't substitute material things for life contentment and connection with others. We try to ignore the realisation that material things have not made us happier, and we renew our efforts and squirrel more and more things away in a desperate attempt to make our lives fulfilled – bigger home; faster, flashier car; higher status at work; a more glamorous look. We buy more and more things and yet we do not have enough. As soon as we catch a breath and look around, the disillusionment returns. Possessions, money and status give us a peak of pleasure and then they dissolve, and we are alone again with our search for living.

People often 'make it' in their forties or fifties, only to realise that their nice car, big home, wardrobe and social connections do not give them happiness. They are not thriving or contented. They do not have peace of mind. But we continue to engage in our endless struggle to reach these external goals anyway. We keep striving to jump through these materialistic hoops and hope that surely life will improve. Eventually, many people start to realise that quality of life and happiness do not depend on what we own or what other people think of us.

> The wonderful world that could be ours
> if we stopped being fearful and greedy.

Interestingly, people who value money more than other goals are less satisfied with their income and their lives as a whole than people who do not value money highly. Actually, valuing money seems to make us *less* happy with the money. This, ironically, is the way that materialism is counterproductive. Another irony is that while meeting our materialistic goals might not give us happiness, if we engage completely in the *journey* of obtaining these goals, we can experience very significant levels of contentment (see Book 3, Part 2 – State of Flow). It is the *pursuit* of the achievement, not the material reward, that gives us contentment.

In every first-world country, we are seeing a startling increase in rates of anxiety and depression. These conditions often start now in teenage years. This is in an era in which 'quality of life' indicators are going up – education, availability to health care, purchasing power, remarkable technological advances – but subjective experience of quality of life and happiness is going down. Why are we increasingly more helpless in facing life, when our ancestors could not have dreamt of the miracles of progress that we are spoilt with? In most of the Western world we cannot blame war or widespread poverty for the anxiety and depression epidemic. The roots of this deteriorating sense of well-being are internal, and each person must work to understand themselves, and to use their own power to start living well.

Our attitudes are driven by a '**hedonic treadmill**'. This is a tendency humans have to adapt rapidly to good things. When something good happens, we inevitably and quickly start taking it for granted. The more we accumulate material accomplishments and possessions, the more our expectations go to the next level. We push hard for something, and then when we get there, the satisfaction that we experience quickly dissolves. We habituate. We need something even better to boost our level of happiness (if this is where we are getting our happiness from). With power and affluence comes escalating expectations, and as expectations rise, the sense of well-being that we are striving so hard for actually slides further from our grasp.

This treadmill continues on and on. It is very sad. We need to understand how to adapt to our newly achieved horizons so we don't get sucked into the belief that *when I get this or that, I will be happy*. We need to see this type of pleasure accurately for what it is, and understand that it is brief and transient satisfaction – not contentment, not joy, not well-being, not happiness. We have to look within ourselves and our connection with others for this level of thriving in life; we can't get it from things or from status.

We need to step away from preconceived ideas of what makes us happy and, like a painter who watches her canvas with care, we have to actually watch what is happening within us and around us and evaluate events based on how they affect us and how we feel. We may then discover that it is our own headspace that facilitates happiness. For example, we can realise that we experience an extraordinary depth of joy in connecting with and supporting others rather than in competing with them for our rung on the status ladder.

Instead of worshipping money and image, to be fully human we need connectedness with ourselves, with others, with our sense of purpose and with society around us. People often end up feeling that their lives have been wasted – that instead of happiness, they experienced years of boredom and anxiety. People can even develop a fear of *being* – a fear that there is no meaning in life (because it has eluded them), and that it is not worth going on with their existence. Nothing makes sense to them. In our culture, we normally don't think about things like meaning and purpose until we are dying. Most people are driving at great speed in life, blind. We are so consumed by egotistical things. Our career, accumulating money and assets, getting a new car that tells others we are successful.

We are mice on a wheel, but we don't actually stop and think: *does the wheel actually get anywhere? Am I thriving? Am I happy? Am I living?* We are not in the habit of standing back and looking at our lives and making clear decisions. If we look at life at all, it is a quick sneak look. But we avoid this reflective moment, fearful of death, fearful of the truth that time is finite; we waste it on distractions and pointless chasing of goals that dissolve in value when we reach them. We are ultimately fearful of the prospect of death, and denial does not serve us well.

The bottom line is that rather than acquiring life's shiny *things*, what actually improves life is the quality of our *experience*. Not in the *having* of things, but in the *living*, in the *doing* of life.

This punchline will continue to become increasingly obvious throughout this series. The skill is simply to learn how everyday life can be made more harmonious and more satisfying. A partial solution won't work here; you have to fully wake up and have clear intention regarding how you live and approach things. Those who have woken up to this – who have escaped the treadmill and quietened the need to meet society's expectations – have been able to improve the quality of their lives regardless of their material conditions. They are satisfied, and they have a way of bringing a force of happiness to those around them.

CHAPTER 12
NEGATIVE THINKING: CONFINED BY OUR OWN MINDS

Negative thinking: it is powerful.

Self-talk is self-explanatory; it's the way you 'talk' to yourself. It involves habitual styles of thinking and the ways you automatically interpret events. Sadly, self-talk can be routinely negative; it is our propensity to be our own worst critic. We are unbelievably hard on ourselves; we slam ourselves with blame and name calling. 'I can't get anything right', 'I'm such an idiot'. We blow this internal monologue way out of proportion, generalising a one-off event to 'always' language. One failure becomes 'I always screw up'.

We would not be so cruel or broad-sweeping in our comments to a friend if she was in our shoes. Negative self-talk involves distorting reality, putting a negative lens or negative bias on ourselves. This negative self-talk goes around and around in our heads, increasing our anxiety or depressive mood. When we are on autopilot we just absorb this negative self-talk as fact; we don't stop and decide how we are going to think about the issue.

If you engage in negative self-talk, your mind would have established false patterns of perception long ago. When your mind thought it couldn't do this or couldn't do that, you started to experience this perception with your emotions and your body. Your false perceptions then limited your ability to do things. Negative self-talk is a soundtrack of negative thoughts that undermines your confidence, your sense of your own abilities, and your ability to relate to others.

Our self-created limitations – does this sound familiar?

I can't do it
I'm not good enough
They think I'm an idiot
I look terrible
I have no talent
I'm going to embarrass myself
I'm going to screw this up
There's something wrong with me
It's too hard
I'm going to fail
No one likes me
I don't deserve it
Nothing goes right for me
What if I can't cope
Need I go on?

I could list hundreds of examples of negative self-talk. Sweeping negative statements like these are false beliefs that are often our baseline – our normal, our familiar. The bad news is that they are sitting there ready to be triggered and go on auto-play. The good news is they are not true. More bad news: they operate as if they *are* true.

We have to change what has previously become our reality. We have to change what we think and say about ourselves and our situation in our own minds. We need to go from being our own bully to our own cheer squad. This is about getting out of our own way; it is about getting rid of the countless negative thoughts that are now a habit. The good news is that once we have the willingness to change, we also have the power to do so. Often coming to understand ourselves is enough to create change, so we are going to take some time to understand where these negative statements come from (with more depth in Book 2 on how negative thoughts and emotions work, and how to overcome them).

CHAPTER 13
PSYCHOLOGICAL ARCHAEOLOGY: 'YOUR ISSUES'

It is essential to work gently with insightful self-inquiry in your daily life to help you discover deeper threads of what triggers your strong emotional reactions. This involves a certain kind of digging – a kind of inner archaeology. You will discover layer upon layer of experiences that have shaped you, such as relationship dynamics and messages from others and interpretations you have made. All of these historical events have worked to shape your experience of yourself, your relationships with others and your experience of the broader world.

These historical events may have generated negative thoughts in you, resulting in your negative self-talk. You might also have a growing sense of alienation and disconnection from others. If you don't feel comfortable within yourself, how can you feel comfortable connecting with others? You might feel estranged and isolated from the world. This is often where psychologists can help. They ask important questions that *you* actually have the answer to. You are learning and becoming an expert about yourself and your inner workings. You need to work gently at the edges here, then progress can lead to a wonderful ripple effect. The momentum of self-awareness then continues and moves to other areas.

> Be an expert on yourself,
> your inner workings.

In mindful self-inquiry, you learn to acknowledge and investigate any thoughts and feelings you'd like to know more about. Though it may be challenging, turning towards your thoughts and your feelings can reveal hidden truths about yourself that help you break free of old patterns, so that your mental health can start to thrive. Acknowledging your fears and inquiring into them will open the door to deeper understanding, and with it, self-compassion, peace and growth. We continue to learn to know ourselves better and as a result we can become more accepting of ourselves. Importantly, this is not as we would like ourselves to be, but as we actually *are*. We need to accept the past, without denying it or discarding it.

When we start to have a clearer sense of our story and how our headspace has been shaped, we can start to see ourselves with clearer perspective. We can start to shift from identifying so much with the role we have been cast in, and distance ourselves from the impact of historical events. This helps create the space for us to sit with issues and events as they are. It helps to deepen our understanding of what underlies, drives and fuels our fears, anger, and sadness. It also grants us the freedom to look at the situation differently. This allows us to choose a different response from the one that was previously scripted for us – a response shaped by the role we used to play. We can play a different role in our story.

> I'm not my past.

We like to think that our situations are largely controlled by our individual choice. The fact, however, is that the most fundamental aspects of our lives are not within our power to choose. We don't choose our parents, our families, our talents, our temperament, our genetic code, or the environment in which we were born. We are also constantly bombarded by other people's behaviour towards us. From birth we unconsciously absorb the behaviours of our family, our community and our culture. We need to learn to become more aware of what these messages from others are and be aware of the expectations and the pressures that we often absorb automatically. We can learn to function with more critical awareness of these influences and make choices for ourselves. We can choose what to take on board, what is helpful, what is not helpful and what we are going to sidestep. How about also cultivating some compassion for ourselves as we deal with these challenges?

CHAPTER 14
NATURE ... NURTURE

To summarise this complex area briefly, we have learnt a lot from the study of the personality of twins and adopted children. Personality is the combination of thought patterns, emotions, behaviour and motivation patterns that define an individual. Identical twins who share genetic code are much more similar in personality than fraternal twins (who only share typical sibling genetic code). Adopted children have also been found to have personalities that are more similar to their biological parents than their adoptive parents. Hundreds of these studies demonstrate that approximately 50% of almost every personality trait is due to genetic inheritance. But this gets more complex when we realise that some traits are highly changeable (like fearfulness and optimism) while others are not very changeable (such as introversion and natural talents like sporting or academic prowess). So nature and nurture both win this debate. How our personality is shaped is a dance between these two important forces.

CHAPTER 15
STORM AND SUNSHINE: PESSIMISM VS OPTIMISM

Optimism is the general tendency to expect positive outcomes, and pessimism is the general tendency to expect negative outcomes. They are on a continuum. This is not a question of which approach is best, as a healthy approach is to balance the two mindsets. They both have something to offer and both have drawbacks. Optimism is associated with hope, however, and has many protective factors.

> *I decided early on that it wasn't worth my time to worry; that it's totally unproductive. I chose to look at the good side of life.*
> John, eighty-three-year-old client

There are well-documented benefits from having an optimistic outlook. Optimism has been linked to resistance to depression, better performance at work (particularly in challenging jobs), and better physical health. Optimistic people have even been found to live longer. Pessimism is the infamous thinking 'this glass is half empty' – the view of ominous grey clouds with no silver lining in sight. Besides making you have a rough time expecting the worst, pessimism is associated with depression, anxiety, sleep problems, high blood pressure, hostility, heart disease and poor self-health care. Optimism and pessimism are beautiful examples of the extraordinary interplay between mind and body. We can influence our recovery from life's setbacks by the ways in which we think and feel about what has afflicted us.

Then there is the self-fulfilling angle to look at. If we perceive others as suspicious and hostile and we approach them in a cold, wary or even hostile way, then they are going to respond to us accordingly. And – surprise, surprise – when they behave in a suspicious and hostile way, our low expectations are confirmed. The opposite is also true. An optimistic attitude towards people will be more likely to draw out their warm and engaging side, thus reinforcing our positive expectations. We enormously shape how people receive us and therefore how they respond to us. What world do we want to engage in? What side of people do we want to draw out? Through these choices we actually create our experience of our world.

While optimism and pessimism are shaped by our personality and our childhood experiences, we can still shape our perception of ourselves and our world, and change where we are on this continuum. At a minimum, we can learn where we sit so that we understand what lens we bring to the situation. Knowing that we have an overly positive or negative perception of an event means that we can work to perhaps moderate our view towards the middle.

Where are *you* on the continuum? Do you know? Where would your loved ones place you?

OPTIMISM  **PESSIMISM**

Let's break it down.

Pessimists believe that bad events are permanent. They often think in a black and white way and use generalisations like 'always' and 'never' ('You never listen to me', 'You always nag'). Pessimists discount positive events and put them down to circumstances ('I just had luck on the day'). Because pessimists see good events as having only a temporary cause, they may actually give up even when they have succeeded. They see a positive event as good luck or a fluke.

Pessimists can see their negatives in life as long term and far reaching. When we view a problem as a crisis, this can then ripple out and make us perceive other areas of our life as equally negative and despairing. We can start to catastrophise and can give up more easily (for example, not go to work because of home stressors). Our lives can therefore more easily unravel. Pessimists can feel long-lasting helplessness as they believe that their troubles will last forever; they undermine everything they do. Pessimists view good news as being restricted to one area of their lives rather than evidence of long-term success. They do not take the pat on the back; they might think, *I did well at that one exam*, rather than appreciating their achievement. Pessimists' explanations for good events stop them from getting on a roll and taking full advantage of their success and achievements.

Optimists believe bad events are temporary, using 'sometimes' and 'lately' as qualifiers ('You sometimes don't hear me', 'I'm struggling with this lately'). Optimists explain good events as a reflection of their strengths and abilities and a positive world around them ('I'm good at this'). As optimists believe good events have more permanent causes, when they have succeeded, they feel rewarded and encouraged, so try even harder next time.

Optimists can put boundaries around a problem. Even when one area of their lives is in crisis (for example, if they are experiencing financial stress), they can put a box around it and keep functioning and keep a consistent buoyant head about the rest of their lives (like their time with family or their work). Optimists tend to interpret their troubles as transient, controllable, and specific to one situation. The optimist can therefore be more resilient and bounce back. Optimists believe good events will have a positive effect on other areas of their lives and are due to their personal strengths ('I'm good at my studies', 'I'm bright'). These explanations help keep successes coming.

Optimists look forward with aspiration. 'What's next? What new thing can I do?' They think in terms of what is possible, not impossible. If you come to something with no preconceived doubts, the whole world can be your canvas. The optimist will smile more, indicating their good humour. They are looking to enjoy life's absurdity and our common humanity. Our world may have grave chapters, but looking for lightness in our experience can soften the serious themes.

I will find a way through.

Here is an irony: there is a downside to optimism and an upside to pessimism. Extreme optimists can show poor attention to detail and selective inattention to unpromising data, which can lead to poorly informed decisions. Optimists can have an unrealistic positive bias in assessing relevant information, which can then lead to errors in judgement. Extreme optimists have been found to have shorter-term financial goals, be poorer at saving, and have less financial self-control.

On the flipside, a certain degree of pessimism has its benefits. Pessimists sometimes make better leaders. Their scepticism can help them plough through difficulties and challenges, because they can imagine possible negative outcomes and develop strategies to prevent them, should they be needed. They don't get as disappointed by what political curveballs are thrown at them, because they're already expecting to be disappointed.

> *We have more possibilities available in each moment than we realise.*
> Thich Nhat Hanh, Buddhist monk and peace activist

With an even broader view than optimism and pessimism, let's talk about our human trait of selective attention to negative feedback. Why do we focus on the rare pieces of negative feedback rather than the majority of positive feedback? Why are we so quick to put our wall up with others? The answer is complex and has to do with scanning for potential threat. If, from 100 pieces of feedback from our peers, we get 99 positive and one negative, what do we focus on? The one piece of negative feedback. If we walked through 100 parks and 99 are safe, but one had a snake, which do we focus on? Answer: the one park with a snake (a relevant example here in Australia!).

This is a survival mechanism: to scan for danger, and to learn from prior experience. This has value, but not with regard to projecting previous bad experiences onto ourselves and other people. We can take a single criticism from others and then launch into a cascade of self-criticism. We also see so many negative news stories, which can give us a distorted and pessimistic view of strangers and the broader world. Innumerable little kindnesses are all too often unnoted and invisible to us. We should look for kindnesses, note them, collect them, create a collage in our minds. This is an accurate picture of human nature, not our biased focus on the rarer negative feedback loops.

CHAPTER 16
'NOT ENOUGH', 'ONE DAY', 'NOT BAD' MANTRAS

We believe there's not enough. No matter what over-abundance of resources we have, we remain under the oppressive spell of 'there's not enough'. We start the day with not enough sleep, then worry that we don't have enough energy or enough time; that the house is not clean enough; that we are not healthy enough, thin enough, funny enough, smart enough, fit enough, educated enough, wealthy enough; that the weekend is not long enough; that we don't have enough clothes to wear. When we are asked, 'How are you?' we routinely answer, 'Busy!'. This is a way of saying, 'Not enough time, not enough energy'. We feel drained, stressed, scared and always on guard. 'Lack of' is so profoundly engrained, we don't stop and check if this 'not enough' mantra is true. This is the lens that shapes every facet of our lives. This 'not enough' lens leads us to feel pessimistic and exhausted and does not drive us to create, to build or to enjoy.

And then there is actively wishing away our lives: 'Only one day to the end of the work week', 'Only one week till my holiday'. When asked what we have been doing, we often answer, 'Not much'. The standard 'How are you?' is routinely answered with, 'Not bad'. We have become out of touch with active exuberance. Our language suggests we are just hanging on, or that our approach to living is a daily grind – or more of a *life* grind!

Young children don't approach their world with 'Not bad, not much'. They tell you stories of things they enjoyed or found interesting. They speak with wonderment. Sadly, this can change when they approach middle childhood and become socialised to not be *too* happy. They also start their own negative self-talk. This book is about turning this around through increasing our mastery of ourselves and going back to our childhood joy.

We have denied the world's loveliness.

It is imperative to talk about and focus on the strengths of our day-to-day life, the degree to which our cup is full, and not on the fact that our cup is not entirely full. We are comfortable asking 'What's wrong?', but not 'What's right?'. But 'What's right?' is actually the question that leads to the new, more joyful story we're trying to create. It leads us to our child wonderment mode. We need to share examples of how our life is improving and growing. By doing so, we share our fascination and passion with living. This attitude is contagious.

CHAPTER 17
FEEL A BIT BROKEN: INTRO TO DEPRESSION AND ANXIETY

We in the Western world are getting more depressed and anxious. Why is this? As mentioned earlier, it seems that this is because we increasingly focus on outside hoops that we are always trying to jump through: image, status, wealth.

The answer is to look inward instead of outward, through self-reflection and control of our consciousness. Mental health allows us a sense of freedom and empowerment; we feel calmer and more capable. When we have an emotional disorder, in contrast, we are restricted in our ability to function. We are constrained, everything is harder work, and we have to compensate for the fears that shape our experience of ourselves and our world. We have problems with our thinking and our brain function.

Why is it that when every other organ in our body gets sick and functions poorly, we get sympathy, but when the problem is with the brain we are often treated as if it is just in our imagination, or that our sickness is a character flaw, a weakness – that we are just not trying hard enough? This is stigma and true ignorance. Perhaps it is a case of 'seeing is believing', and many who have not had anxiety or depression just struggle to understand it. This of course creates more pressure and isolation for people who are suffering from mental illness. What really makes no sense is that almost half of the population will experience a mental health disorder in their lifespan. Does this not educate us to the nature and struggle we humans routinely face with these brain-based problems?

If you live in a world of dark clouds that affect your mood, your sense of yourself and your future, and you feel minimal pleasure and flattened energy, then you are probably feeling depressed. If you live in the world where you are routinely tormented with 'What if this happens, what if that happens?' then you are probably experiencing anxiety. This is not okay for you; this is not good enough. You need to be free of this depressed and/or anxious state.

People who get professional support and guidance routinely say they should have got help earlier. You can learn from them. Reach out for help – and do it sooner, not later. We need to clear something up, however: there is a difference between feeling depressed and depression, and feeling anxiety and having an anxiety disorder. Feeling depressed and anxious are emotional states that are linked to our thinking (our behaviours interweave in there too). When our anxious head has become our predominant style of thinking and feeling for over six months, then it has become chronic, and it may meet diagnostic criteria for **generalized anxiety disorder**. When we stay in this depressive outlook and emotional state without having a sustained break from it we then may have **major depression**. The diagnoses are just ways of communicating how chronic and entrenched these horrible mood states have become for us, and the degree of their impact on our lives.

It is human nature for our brain to go to the negative when it comes to danger. Our mind is often a soundtrack of depressive and anxious self-talk that comes from the way our brains are wired. These brain habits stem from hundreds of thousands of years ago, when searching for the negative helped us see threats. This caution helped us survive physical dangers. Is that a snake, or is that a stick? Watch out for that sabre-toothed tiger! We were always looking around for danger. When our prehistoric ancestors then developed language, we started to translate those feelings of danger, but we got the language wrong. We have transformed our searching for physical danger into a sense of psychological danger – of negative self-talk like 'I'm not good enough', 'They're judging me', 'I'll be rejected', 'I can't do it', 'I'm a failure'.

This need to change our mindsets is a universal issue, a global human problem. Psychologist Rick Hanson points outs that our brains have evolved to be like 'Velcro for bad experiences and Teflon for good experiences'. So true. We have to realise that we need to consciously and intentionally reverse this tendency. We truly behave as if we expect others and ourselves to be perfect, because any imperfection triggers our tendency for negative thinking. And when we or others are then inevitably not perfect, we whip ourselves into a frenzy of negative self-talk … and anxiety and depressive mood is the result.

> 'I'm not good enough', 'They're judging me', 'I'll be rejected', 'I can't do it', 'I'm a failure'.

Anxiety and depression are different expressions of the same thing: fear. Fear that we are inadequate in our own eyes or in the opinions of others, and fear we are going to fail or have failed. Fear that we are out of control, that we are helpless, that our future is hopeless. Fear of our vulnerabilities and our messy humanness. Sometimes anxiety and depression present together, or we can have one primary and one secondary diagnosis. When we have depression, because we are so depleted and dark in our mood, we can feel anxious that we are not capable of managing in the world. Or we can have primary anxiety, and from the sheer volume of negative reflections about the past and negative anticipation about the future, we can start to feel depressive. The overlap of these two conditions is high, at approximately 85–90%.

With regard to mental health struggles, it is crucial to keep crystal clear that *we are not our sickness*. We are not our depression. We are not our anxiety. This is a state that we are experiencing. It is one facet of our life. We work to make the ugly clouds pass and then we continue on to the next chapter of our lives. Sometimes the medical model can over-medicalise anxiety and depression and give people the impression that this is a label that will be with them for the rest of their lives. But these are not permanent diagnoses; they are episodes in our lives.

Our job is to make these episodes as short as possible, and to learn and become stronger through them. Usually we need a skilled person to be our backboard, to shine a light on our patterns, and to provide supportive scaffolding to help us get back on our feet. Psychotherapy is a tool to push us through these episodes as quickly as possible, and with the most self-learning that we can muster. Psychotherapy is very goal-directed; it is about increasing self-awareness and creating growth and change. It encompasses many areas, including learning about and skilling up our thoughts, emotions and behaviours, acceptance of self and areas of suffering, self-compassion and other forms of compassion, and mindfulness skills to increase our psychological adaptability.

Modern anti-anxiety and anti-depressant medications are proving to be remarkably effective. One problem with this, however, is that because medication helps us so much, we can start seeing anxiety and depression as purely physical illnesses. We can start to think that healing is something that happens to us rather than a process in which we are active participants. We can develop a passive attitude in our healing, believing that taking a pill will be sufficient to relieve our suffering. Traditional medicine can therefore inadvertently promote a sense of helplessness in the face of mental illness. There can be a tendency to defer to doctors to fix us, rather than taking responsibility and doing the legwork to fix ourselves. We can put our hands up and take no responsibility for what has got us to this point, and what we can do – and need to do – to dig ourselves out of the hole that we are in. We can depend on medication rather than learn how to function better psychologically.

We should not just take medication and then sit on our hands. Medication does not create new learning, more self-awareness, psychological strengthening or interpersonal skills. The only way to overcome the sense of powerlessness that is core to anxiety and depression is a determination to overcome discouragement and fear. We have an obligation to learn to have greater control over our lives. While medication definitely has its therapeutic role to play with severe and chronic depression and anxiety, the continuing importance of psychotherapy in learning skills to change thoughts, emotions and behaviours remains core to psychological recovery. The key is creating change and increasing choice in our pursuit of purpose, contentment and joy.

CHAPTER 18
ANXIETY: 'WHAT IF, WHAT IF, WHAT IF ...'

Millions of people live with stress and anxiety every day – nearly 30% of the population at some point in their lifespan. That is a big number. This can revolve around daily stress, work pressures, relationship communication breakdown, difficult life events, health concerns, and a bucket of negative self-talk. There is rarely a single cause. Anxiety means constantly anticipating spot fires in our lives, waiting for the next inevitable fireball, and the next and the next.

Actually, anxiety is the anticipation of a future problem or an over-analysis and catastrophising of our past. What if, what if, what if, continue, continue, continue. You are going in circles, going nowhere.

When we frequently live in highly elevated levels of anxiety, we are constantly flushing our system with the stress hormone cortisol. This has a ripple effect throughout many systems in our bodies. It can affect the whole plumbing pathway – from digestion to bowel release – and it can cause indigestion, heartburn, bloating, poor absorption of key nutrients, irritable stomachs, diarrhoea and constipation. High cortisol levels can cause chronic inflammation and reduce bone density. When stressed, some people gain weight, while others shed weight.

Anxiety is largely fuelled by the critical part of yourself – the part that wants to run a commentary telling you that you are not doing well. Your critical self has an opinion about all of your actions; it chatters away, like a bully in your mind, with never-ending comments telling you that you are inadequate. Your critical self is always correcting and undermining you and gets in the way of your performance.

One example of how this critical self can get out of control is perfectionism. We seek out control and perfect standards to avoid feeling anxiety, but ironically this approach only *causes* the pressure and anxiety that we are trying to avoid. This hypervigilant approach to our worlds and our own headspace becomes normal to us; it snowballs and spirals to a point where we are drowning in it. This is an example of our tendency to focus on the *content* of our thoughts, not the *process* of our thoughts.

Let me explain. If we keep cooking soufflés and time and time again the soufflés do not turn out well, we would not criticise the individual soufflés; we would look at our cooking approach, our technique. There is clearly something wrong with our cooking technique to have a negative outcome time and time again. It is the same with our anxiety. It's not helpful to keep focusing on the things that we are anxious about (our soufflés); it is more helpful to look at our approach to thinking (our cooking technique) that keeps resulting in our anxious thoughts.

Anxiety is a mirror that reflects what we personally value. We have to value something to fear losing it or losing control of it. For example, if we overly care about other people's opinions of us, then we fear criticism; if we overly need to succeed to feel good about ourselves, then we have a fear of failure; if we overly need assurance that others will be there for us, then we fear abandonment. Anxiety is actually the looking glass to see what makes us tick, what is our kryptonite, what we fear losing the most. Usually anxiety is a lack of connection with ourselves. It is a sense that something is missing, that we feel incomplete. This is what has us looking outward for reassurance.

OUR PAST, OUR FUTURE

Anxiety is about our past and our future, not our *now*. We go around and around like a broken record saying the famous anxious words 'what if'. We worry about what we or someone else has done in the past, we micro-analyse behaviour, and we worry about the future, rehearsing over and over what could go wrong, as we think about contingency plans. These are just narratives that we have created about our past and our future. This is called

ruminating. We are mice on the wheel, putting in a lot of energy, but not getting anywhere, just getting worn out and despondent. We rush around in a frenzy, competing with others, jumping through hoops. By looking away from the now, we are missing what is happening for us in this moment.

It is the urgency and the rushing to seek out answers and our assurances from our past and our future that makes us unaware of the 'me' that exists right now. The *me* that *is* actually good enough despite all of the negative messages that we tell ourselves. Our focus on the unknown, our lack of guarantees of our ability to cope in the future and our lack of knowledge about what other people think about us is what fuels our anxiety. It is vital that we regularly check in with ourselves to see how we are travelling. This cuts through the rumination. This gentle moment with ourselves where we reflect on our current needs, demands and joys is very grounding and re-orientating. When we are in the now, we are not in the past or the future, and we are not able to ruminate on repeat.

Ironically, people with anxiety are often excellent if genuine stressors actually happen. Current stressors take us out of our anxious thoughts about the past and the future, because we simply do not have the time or headspace for them. When we attend to genuine fear and catastrophes in the now, we experience a different type of tension; we are hypervigilant to the threats that face us now, not the fears in our heads.

Another sad irony is that our personal irrational fears often distract us from actual fundamental and rational fears on our doorstop such as environmental degradation and violation of civil liberties. We worry about past conversations and plan for largely superficial things, when more profound problems don't even register in our minds. Our prioritising is upside down. That's like worrying about a chipped nail when your house is on fire.

One reason we withdraw our attention from our actual, profound global problems is that they may seem well beyond our individual ability to have an influence. This is not true; we can be part of the butterfly effect; we can all create ripples in awakening global attitudes. Small choices from many move mountains here. What we need to work towards is the ability to analyse our fears and keep them in perspective, while keeping the need for broader global issues clearly in our view. Our awareness that life will inevitably involve random chapters of misfortune and our awareness of our mortality crystallise our need to savour the current moment and have gratitude.

Choose not to have your current joy drained by self-created regrets from the past or fears for the future.

WHO IS VULNERABLE TO ANXIETY?

Some of us are especially vulnerable to anxiety. Obviously, there are the shy folk, who are timid until they warm up and feel secure. They can easily overthink as the world can sometimes be especially daunting for them and social interactions may not come naturally.

If we seek perfection in our imperfect world, then we are also walking straight into anxious patterns. To compensate for this sense of vulnerability, we tend to place a strong emphasis on control and a desire to create order. When we feel that we cannot achieve this control, our anxiety grows further, and this negative spiral continues. With our attempts to gain control we overthink our future and our past. We feel pressured, we feel frustrated and we feel disempowered. We are failing to control our world.

While perfectionists can have skills that make them thrive in pedantic and detail-orientated occupations (like surgeons, pilots, administrative auditors, engineers), it is these rigid qualities that can cause them to struggle in their personal and relationship worlds. They *need* to be controlling in their work world – but somehow they need to change gear to be less controlling in their personal lives. This is very difficult. Ironically, with anxiety there is a paradox. We only gain control in our intimate relationships if we relinquish control. This is the paradox of affection. When we allow our other person the freedom to be themselves and to come to us with affection, we can create a relationship in which we have positive influence, we both have a voice, and we both feel safe to listen and be open to each other.

GET YOUR HEAD AROUND IT

Great news: studies have found that just saying the simple statement, 'I'm anxious' – just identifying that this is how you are feeling – will make you less anxious. Why? Because it activates a different part of your brain. (If you want to know the anatomical terms, it activates the more analytical **pre-frontal lobe** instead of the 'reacting' **amygdala**). You then start to become aware that it is your *anxious approach* that is playing a large role here; it is not the issue itself causing your negative emotional state. This is not about *reacting* but *accepting* that you feel anxious. There is no point protesting and saying, 'I should not be anxious', because you *are* feeling anxious.

Perhaps the best skill is the realisation that the answer isn't to turn away from our anxiety, but to turn towards it. We usually try to run away from our anxiety, but this can just make it grow. We need to get in touch with our concerns and learn to work with them so that they aren't so paralysing. Although you can't always control or eliminate stressors, you can engage with them differently. The key is mindfully exploring what may be influencing your relationship with the challenges in your life and examining what works and what doesn't work in dealing with them.

Another helpful hint for getting our heads around our anxiety is to actually label what it is that we fear about our past or our future. Anxiety is an emotion and thinking pattern that is secondary to fear. So, what is the primary fear issue? Peel it back. Talk to the true issue, the true cause. Then we have a chance to ground ourselves and self-soothe with some rational self-talk. We can reason our way through the problem state. When we can sit with our anxiety, we can strengthen through it; we can expand. When we become aware and stay with our anxiety, it eventually fades and takes a back seat; it reduces to a manageable and livable size. When we treat our anxious state with kindness and respect, we become desensitised to our anxiety.

It won't happen immediately; it may take a bit of time, patience, practice and intention, but what a wonderful investment, to actually create a release from our anxious themes. By sitting in these uncomfortable states of anxiety, the energy in the emotion becomes exhausted. You go *into* the pain that is anxiety. You sit with it, in it. You decide to stay with the uncomfortable. It takes bravery and determination. It's a game of chicken: who is going to win, you or your anxiety? This is our modern-day version of wisdom, staring down our modern-day anxiety.

ANXIOUS ABOUT BEING ANXIOUS

We even get anxious about being anxious. Perhaps this is the worst form of anxiety. Humans are the only animals on the planet capable of knowing they are anxious.

The key is not to fear the fear, and to see anxiety for what it is. This makes an extraordinary difference. If we just accept that if we feel anxious in the future, we will deal with it *then*, then we won't worry about future anxiety now. Having anxiety is unpleasant, but it is not dangerous. It is not catastrophic. There is a time frame; it will resolve, and it is not going to hurt you. As unpleasant as extreme anxiety is, it will eventually go. You will recover. You will be okay, and you can use your knowledge and skills to address your concerns when they happen. Full stop. No need to worry.

Our brain works to problem-solve; this is the function of our neurological machine. If something is wrong, we try to fix it, so we chew over issues from our past and our future, over and over again; we ruminate. Rumination gives the false impression that we are doing something about the problem. Anything is better than not knowing. We would rather be like a mouse on a wheel; we would rather ruminate and have cyclical thoughts, trying to achieve a fix for our problems, than to sit and look at our underlying fears.

INTERPRET AS EXCITEMENT

How are anxiety and excitement different? They are actually very similar; they both make us feel nauseated and cause our heart to quicken and our stomach to flutter. We can actually *choose* to interpret anxiety as excitement. If we decide the situation is actually exciting, we can have fun with it. This is about repackaging anxiety so that we get on board; it is about taking control, finding the positive and focusing on it. We may be anxious about doing a public talk, for example. We can flip our interpretation and see it as a challenge, an opportunity to achieve our purpose, and we can focus on the relief and exhilaration of having it over once complete. We can determinedly sell it to ourselves that it is excitement that we are feeling.

Your reasoning in doing this is true and accurate; it is just that you are putting emphasis on these positive components; you are self-soothing; you are actively helping yourself through a difficult time. You can improve your performance; you can find fun in what you are doing. This is your responsibility to yourself. The hero uses her fear. Courage means fearing something and doing it anyway. It's what you do with your fear that matters.

HAVE A SENSE OF HUMOUR ABOUT THE ABSURDNESS OF OUR ANXIETY. GET BORED BY THE SHEER REPETITION.

We can decide to become bored by our anxiety. It is the same conversation with ourselves on repeat, and repeat, and repeat. If we had the same conversation with someone else, we would quickly get bored. If we can zoom out our lens and look at the broader picture, we can also see how ridiculous we often are.

Notice when you are sweating the small stuff: expecting others to read your mind; getting frustrated with your kids for not having adult maturity yet; rushing to deadlines when you have put yourself in that situation; blowing small irritations into mountains, like when your partner won't fold washing the way you want them to. Notice when you're just so scared of change that you don't fix an obvious problem.

This list is endless and somehow we always pull through. On our deathbeds will we care about any this? No. Actually, in a month, a week or even a day, will we care about the thing we are worried about in this moment? Usually not. We will strain to remember any of it. Our focus will shift, and the world will keep turning.

Of course, there are genuine and meaningful stressors that create anxiety, but these are not the sort that repeat day after day after day. So, if we decide to get bored and see the humour in our anxiety, in the messiness, absurdness and weirdness of life, then the power of that anxiety diminishes. This skill of keeping things in perspective is the skill of stepping away from your mental traffic. Instead of desperately grasping through life, we can sit quietly with ourselves. This is the wisdom of finding beauty in the imperfection of life. We can then see many broader truths to life.

OUR ANXIOUS BODIES

We feel anxiety in our bodies. It is a very physical emotion. It activates our stress response; our senses and nervous system are alert, we become irritable and less naturally patient. We are especially alert to any smells that we have previously learnt to associate with threat and stress. We are not as astute with smells as our canine friends, but we do become alert to trigger smells nevertheless. Numerous medical conditions have been associated with stress and anxiety, including cancer, cardiovascular disease, and reproductive disorders.

We don't want the physical costs of anxiety, so what can help release this physical anxious tension? Physical exercise releases physical tension, so the more we stress, the more we should exercise. This can be intensive exercise to flush out our negative stress hormone, cortisol, or more relaxing exercise to self-soothe and ground us in mindful calmness. Our core muscles need a special shout-out here. Research has discovered there are links between the nerve cells in our core muscles and our glands that produce the hormones that regulate our response to stress (adrenal glands). How we look after our core muscles either helps or hinders our stress levels. Exercise that consciously activates the core (like yoga and pilates) therefore helps our neurological pathways that control stress. The mindful breathing techniques used in these practices also release stress built up within the body.

Another hot tip is massage. Massage therapy decreases our cortisol (stress hormone) levels and increases our levels of serotonin (the hormone that is our natural mood stabiliser, reduces depression and regulates anxiety). Out with the bad, in with the good neurochemicals. Massage also reduces muscle tension in the stress points and increases blood circulation to the brain. I personally have the choice between monthly massages or fortnightly migraines: not a hard choice for me to make. Prevention is great for stress-related physical symptoms and, in the case of massage, very enjoyable.

PHOBIAS

The human brain is pretty amazing. However, basically everything that goes right can go wrong. An amazing array of phobias and specific fears are examples of this. These are irrational and disabling fears that can build up to panic symptoms. **Phobias** are divided into **specific phobias** and **social phobia**.

Specific phobias
There are hundreds of specific triggers that can create specific phobias. We can develop a specific phobia in relation to pretty much anything as it is a learnt conditioned response. Some common examples are a fear of spiders, snakes, dogs, insects, heights, thunder, confined or crowded spaces, darkness, injections, blood, being alone, flying, riding an elevator, driving, choking, drowning, etc.

Agoraphobia is a specific phobia worth a particular mention. It is a fear of being trapped and not being able to escape from a situation. These fears may involve being in public places or lifts, as an example. Sufferers are always aware of their exit plan. They stay near doorways. When we experience panic attacks, the thought we have is *I need to escape; I feel trapped*. This really is a survival instinct from our ancestors coming through. Agoraphobia often begins with this fearful thought and leads to panic attacks.

Social phobia
Social phobia involves a profound and paralysing fear of public humiliation. Sufferers fear being singled out and judged by others in social situations. Large social gatherings are terrifying. This is not shyness, it is terror.

I used to have a specific phobia whereby I feared milk. It is an odd one. In my twenty years of psychology practice, I haven't seen this in anyone else, but I'm sure I can't be alone. At nine years old, while at an event where there were baby farm animals, enthusiastic little Kirsty was the first to volunteer to milk a goat. I was then invited to taste the milk directly from the udder. Were they joking? I shall never know. I thought, *No thanks*, but my Dad thought it would be a great educational experience. So, under pressure, I had a taste and was struck by its warmth and weird, wrong consistency. I associated it with warm mucus.

From then on, I developed a bizarre milk phobia. I would only drink icy cold milk. If the milk was not icy cold, I would feel nausea and want to vomit. It was an intense and powerful physical response. This was a problem. I was also hypervigilant to anyone else drinking milk that was not icy and would assess the coldness of their milk. When I would observe that someone had milk that was not icy cold anymore, I would experience the acute nausea and feel an anxiety attack coming. I would have to leave abruptly. This affected me in cafés, people's houses, and work functions. When working (as a psychologist!) at an accident and emergency hospital, I actually left work because a work colleague turned up with a milk drink. I calculated where the closest shop was, where the car park was ... and no, I concluded that the milk could not be ice cold. I was working to calm myself down from my phobia, when I saw her take a sip, put the lid back on, and put the milk drink back into her bag. Well, I was out of there. Ridiculous, I know. But phobias usually are.

Do I have the phobia now? No. Not a hint of it. I just have a sense of humour about it now. How? I can take no credit. I had my first child, and along came the warm breast milk. Flooding, exposure; *I* was now the cow! And I was over it in a day. A lot of gratitude for the wonderful distraction of a baby to soothe the transition back to the real world on this issue. I am glad that I have had a phobia. Now I have informed empathy for hundreds of clients that I have met with this struggle. I feel really, *really* frustrated by people who don't understand and taunt others who are struggling with phobias (like the brother who puts a grasshopper on his sister even in adulthood). I would not erase this experience for all the growth it has given me.

By the way, I hate to say it, but I have another phobia now. After twenty years of working with clients recounting their horrific motor vehicle accidents, I now have a full blown 'car passenger phobia' from the vicarious trauma. Lots of fun! I'm working through it, and I have improved tremendously. I let my lovely Jon drive and daily face my fear, neutralising its potency.

Baby steps.

Anxiety attacks and panic attacks are the physical and psychological response to acute anxiety and phobias. We humans hate feeling out of control. Therefore, anxiety attacks and panic attacks can be even more complex and confusing when we don't have conscious awareness of what we are stressed about, or what the trigger has been. We are going to explore this and how to reverse these horrible avalanches of anxiety in Book 2, Chapters 7 and 14 to 16, and Book 3, Chapter 18.

Whatever our fears, our job is to learn our thinking processes, our emotional reactions, our physical stress response and our avoidant behaviours. We then need to face our fears with buckets of self-education, a strategic game plan and therapeutic support. And yes, we can face our fears and conquer them, whether they be specific phobias, social phobia or their close cousin, obsessive-compulsive disorder. We need to learn about distress tolerance where we learn to remain in anxiety-provoking situations until our fear literally hits saturation point and it reduces to a manageable level. We learn that our fear is not really an emergency, and that we are actually safe. This is a challenge as we have to learn to sit with our triggers.

The good news is that we go with baby steps first, working with the easiest challenge and only working up to our harder challenges as we rack up our successes. Ironically, we get to watch as these larger challenges actually shrink before us. It seems counterintuitive to seek out our own discomfort situations, but this is the essential experimental design for overcoming specific anxiety triggers. This is about learning that you actually can become more empowered; you can do things you never dreamt that you could do. You take control of your anxiety.

CHAPTER 19
DEPRESSION

Depression = learnt hopelessness + learnt helplessness towards ourselves, our future and our world.

Depression often has the theme of obsessing over what should have been. We have regrets and remorse about our past and a sense of hopelessness and helplessness about ourselves, others and our world in the future. When we are depressed, our sad mood, our inability to concentrate and our loss of energy cause us to withdraw from people. The activities and social contact that used to give us pleasure no longer do. Our ability to 'adult' well, to interpersonally relate and to work or study is greatly impacted. A small subgroup of depressed people even lose their will to live. We become so debilitated in our daily functioning that we can lose touch with reality, and this prevents us from engaging freely in our world.

The antidote to depression is perhaps choice and a sense of humour about the absurdness of life. The more choice we have available to us, the happier we are likely to be.

While outside forces (like illness or lack of job promotion) can restrict our choices, the primary restriction is from our own negative self-talk. We can also be limited by our fear of change and avoidance of risk.

Healthy self-talk helps us to embrace our expectations of how we want to live our life and who we want to be. It helps us to keep our headspace in perspective, and this is where a great sense of humour can be useful. Our trials and tribulations really shrink and are often ridiculous when we take an 'in proportion to life' perspective. We need to throw away societal pressures that impact on our sense of worth, and false and superficial thinking habits that we have adopted. We need to identify ways we have been programmed to have an unhealthy idea of our worth. We need to learn that we do not need to jump through societal hoops or achieve to be loved. When we are loving to others, we open ourselves up to so many opportunities to feel loved by others.

Energy goes up or down based on depressed mood and happy mood. When we receive great news, we have a burst of energy; we are bounding and bubbling over. We understand this and it makes sense to us in the moment. So why does the opposite – a severe deterioration in energy with depression – not make sense to us? It's hard work wading through the dark cloud. Our heads are black, our outlook towards ourselves and our future is dim, our energy is zapped. Moving our body feels like moving mountains. Low energy is a physical expression and symptom of depressed mood. It is real. It is concrete. When people who are severely depressed struggle to get out of bed, they are often misunderstood and judged as lazy. But their fatigue is like the fatigue of a severe flu when you feel like you have been hit by a bus.

Instead of judging, we need to understand the courage and sheer willpower of depressed people who put one foot in front of the other and push through the day. If we could see on a neon sign on their foreheads that they are requiring 110% effort to achieve the basics, while non-depressed people may be only needing 30% effort for the same activity, then we would be filled with admiration, not judgement.

For severe depression, the first treatment is called **behavioural activation**: the achievement of getting out of bed, having a shower and going for a walk to get the newspaper. Not because you want the newspaper, but because this is the rehabilitation type work you have to do. This is why having children is a protective factor for depression. Parents have no choice but to get out of bed and care for their young. This obliged movement is a positive step towards recovery.

If we think about depression in our prehistoric days, this lack of energy makes sense. Imagine this: a member of the community is acutely depressed or grieving but they have no language to communicate. What do they do? They curl up and behave as if their batteries are removed. They curl up under a tree, they avoid their people, they don't care to feed themselves and they just sleep. What a clever way to communicate to the tribe that they are not okay, and that the tribe needs to care for them. The diminished energy of depression is a clever communication tool to say, 'Hey, seriously not okay here'. We have come a long way from the old stoic approach of just 'soldier on'. But we have a way to go. A lot more compassion is needed all round.

Many people say 'I have depression' as if they are resigned to a life sentence. I guess this is a depressed view of depression. Fair enough! They are resigning themselves to 'Oh well, I'm going to sit in my hole my whole life'.

But depression is not a life sentence. It does not define us; it is not our self-identity. Depressive mood is a current mood state or episode, not a life role that is cast for you.

CHAPTER 20
LIVING ON AUTOPILOT

Most of us live in a fog. We are on autopilot. We travel in a passive mode, largely reactive to our world, not proactive. Dragging our feet in a habitual pattern. It is only when we learn to observe our inner thoughts and feelings closely that we realise we have been living in this heavy fog of automatic, unconscious thinking and habits. Without this reflective living we can become confined by our own minds.

Socrates famously said, 'The unexamined life is not worth living.' These are strong words, but it is a clear truth that we create our own limitations through living unreflectively. How can we live vibrantly and thrive if we are walking around in our sleep? Because we are half asleep, we don't experience the world fully; we automatically do things we think we have to do, and the way that we have always done them. We often don't even like or agree with our familiar patterns of thinking and behaving, but we repeat them mindlessly.

Human beings are creatures of habit, which has its advantages in many procedural areas of daily function. But habit is not a friend to coping with stress. When you are operating on autopilot, you're not likely to be aware of your reactions to stress and anxiety, let alone be in a position to choose the optimal approach. We often react impulsively in habitual ways based on our past conditioning. Conditioning is the process in which a set of behaviours have been shaped and learnt because of a history of reinforcement (positive and negative). On autopilot, we may not even recognise that we have a space between the stimulus and response in which we can choose a different response. When patterns become entrenched, it can be difficult to change them. Mindful self-inquiry helps us see more clearly what we're doing and, more importantly, why. As you become more self-aware and contemplate your choices, you'll become more aware of the possibilities open to you.

Do you believe that your past behaviours and ways of relating to yourself and your world will just continue unchanged? If you believe that your past determines your future, you are giving yourself an excuse to be passive and just let old patterns continue. This creates an apathetic approach to living, where you are in the passenger seat, not the driver's seat, and yet you are probably aware that you are not happy about how the journey is going for you.

CHAPTER 21
THE 'SHOULDS': DRAGGING YOURSELF THROUGH LIFE

'Should' is a swear word. I am being very serious and literal here. It is the worst sort as it causes the most harm through a piling up of guilt. It reduces our self-compassion for our many messy life errors. Whenever we put the word 'should' at the beginning of a sentence we set ourselves up to feel obliged to do the act; we feel pressured and we drag ourselves forward to engage.

I want to do ... I shall do ... I plan to do ... I intend to do ... these statements enforce that we are choosing, that we feel empowered, that we are in the driver's seat.

I 'should' do ... says, 'I feel obliged, guilty; I am failing if I don't do it.' 'Should' weakens resolve; 'should' places us in the passenger seat. 'Should' takes away our ownership of the action and creates a negative event. It saps us of energy and passion for the task.

It is extraordinary how often we operate from a belief system that is filled with countless inner rules and judgements about how we, others and the world 'should' be.

When our 'shoulds' are not met we feel resentment and anger towards others and guilt and self-loathing towards ourselves. 'I should clean the house', 'My workmate should get all the data entry done', 'My husband should know that bothers me'. We create a negative attitude straight away. Our behaviour that follows is not likely to be overly healthy and nurturing to ourself or to others. Often – really often – we have an inner rule or judgement that others should do something in a certain way – in *our* way – and they ought to be telepathically aware of this. We are imposing ourselves on them. But they are their own person, with their own background, composition of self, and agenda. They are not our employees, nor clones of us. Yet we expect them to follow our 'shoulds'.

Except for the extreme violations of moral code (like 'one should not harm children'), let's literally ban the word 'should' from everyday use. Treat it as the worst swear word that you know. It is a word that harms you, saps you of energy and creates an instant negative relationship between you and the intended action. Catch yourself when you go to say 'should' and replace it with a phrase of choice: 'I want to' or 'It is my priority to'. You are about to dive into self-discovery here. The revolution of how often and how much you are driven by these inner rules and judgements shall be extraordinary. The more you struggle to not use the word 'should', the more you will benefit from this self-awareness and mindset renovation. You are choosing to relate to yourself, others and the world differently – with a healthy head.

CHAPTER 22
TRAIN THE MIND

The brain is an organ, just like the heart and lungs, that has a specific function. One of its functions is to process our thoughts. We tend to have little awareness of the incessant and relentless activity of our own thoughts and how much we are driven by them. This is not surprising, given that we hardly ever stop and observe our mind directly to see what it is up to.

OBSERVE YOURSELF: EXPERIMENT TIME

Let's do a small experiment. Put on an alarm for one minute. Grab a piece of paper and pen. Press *start* on the timer. I want you to simply make a dot on the page every time you have a thought.

Example of random thoughts:
Is this what I am supposed to do? = write a dot •
I can hear the air-conditioning = write a dot •
What will I have for lunch? = write a dot •
Why did Ella look at me like that? = write a dot •
Is a minute up? = write a dot •
= • • • • • • • • • • • •

One minute finishes.

How many dots did you have? In my experience approximately 12-14 thoughts per minute is common. Were you more or less? Was it weird to just sit and notice your thoughts?

Punchline: what happened to your thoughts after you drew the dot? Most people say the thought went away and they were just sitting; perhaps they were having their next thought. The interesting thing is that when we draw the dot, we are acknowledging the thought (without any intention of engaging in the thought – because of the exercise condition). And this is exactly what we can do in real time. When we acknowledge our thoughts and choose not to engage, they do usually move on by, down our river of consciousness.

Our thoughts are ideas that pop into our head. They are based on many things: our assumptions, our belief systems, our previous experiences and lessons from our world experience, our fears. Our thoughts can come from fact or complete fiction. Our thoughts continue to pop into our heads and flow through our conscious awareness. They are like songs on a play list – some are new, but most are programmed to repeat as they are on our 'popular' or 'most played' list. When they have been played many times before, they are flagged to keep being selected and played.

But here is the thing: they are just thoughts. They are just ideas, creations, impulses, desires, judgements.

Thoughts are not fact. *We are not our thoughts.*

Just because a thought has popped into your mind does not mean that you have to agree with it, subscribe to it, or align yourself with it. Just like we engage in people-watching, we need to do 'thought watching', and realise that thoughts are just ideas or information about our 'issues', our priorities, our fears, our previous pain, our most-played list. This is about honouring each moment. Each moment is important information about how your head works and an important opportunity to get even healthier in our thinking patterns. Each moment is an opportunity to shape our future moments. Just as we are distant from the people who we 'people watch', we need to create distance from our thoughts to 'thought watch'.

One very big hurdle is the power and the sting of some of our thoughts. Just like a bully knows where the vulnerable spots are, so too does our own mind when we are brainstorming ways to create self-doubt and self-criticism. We go for the soft, vulnerable areas. We can see accusations from others as ungrounded much more easily than when the accusations come from us. We can struggle to distance ourselves from our thoughts. Our negative self-talk usually contains cruel distortions that are so out of perspective that they have no basis. This negative self-talk has its roots somewhere: childhood, peer or family conflicts, critical tone from parents, or tricky 'problem people' in our lives. We have usually had our negative self-talk for so long that it has become the norm and we have started to believe the cruel messages.

CHAPTER 23
RIVER OF CONSCIOUSNESS

Our thoughts travel along a river of consciousness. You can become aware of a thought as it arises and as it eventually passes by. In the same way that you can sit by a stream and watch leaves float by, you can become aware of your thoughts as they come and go. Instead of being actually in the river with your thoughts and hopping from one to another, absorbing them as they come, you need to stand on the riverbank, perhaps on a hill with a bit of distance and therefore a better perspective, and watch the thoughts flow through your consciousness. Be interested in how fast the river flows; is it a gentle river with a gentle rhythm? Or is it more like rapids, with your thoughts firing at you, fast and furious, often piling over and into each other? You might be frantically trying to keep up with the fast pace, feeling like you are drowning with the speed of your thinking.

Next, as you 'thought watch', study the themes that you notice. What do the patterns from these passing thoughts tell you about yourself and your issues? For example, are you frequently having negative thoughts comparing yourself with others? What does this theme tell you about your own lack of confidence? Do you notice that these thoughts are not triggered when you are with a different group of people? What does it say about *you*, if you feel different with this other group? Why do you feel more comfortable with them or more confident about yourself? What are your issues here? What are your patterns? What do you know about yourself from this? Just watching your thoughts gives you all the information you need to study yourself.

CHAPTER 24
CHOOSE TO DANCE OR 'PASS': YOUR THOUGHTS

How do you practise not reacting to your thoughts? First of all, the key is to decide which thoughts to put any effort into. You might like to think about them as the thoughts you are choosing to dance with.

I've found the sushi train analogy to work well with clients. Here it is. When you are seated at a sushi train restaurant, you look at the sushi as it comes along the conveyor belt, then see something you want to choose. You decide if it is what you want. You are not obliged to take all of the sushi and eat it all just because it is coming past you. No, you are selective. And if the sushi does not look of quality you do not choose it. It is the same with your thoughts: you watch your thoughts come along the river, like the sushi train, and you respond to your thoughts with skill. You can choose to observe the thought, and let it pass, or choose to engage and allow the thought into your mind and your world.

THE PROCESS IN BROAD STROKES

1. Realise the thought is not necessarily fact or true. You do not have to agree with the thought; you do not even have to engage with the thought. You do not need to pick up the thought. You can just observe the thought and let it float past.

2. You decide if the thought is factual and true, and whether it is helpful or dysfunctional. Consider whether the thought is quality and a keeper or whether you will say, 'Pass'. You can even decide that the thought is true and reasonable, but it is not what you want to engage in at that moment. It's not a good time. For example, you might be sad or infuriated over a recent break-up but you have done a lot of processing of this and you do not want to keep going in circles; it is time to move on and get him/her out of your head. Or you are about to go to work and it is not a good time to get upset. So you can observe your break-up thought and leave it alone in the river, and let it float by. You can observe the thought and acknowledge it, but you do not need to pick it up and absorb it then and there.

   Another example is that you might realise you are anxious about starting a new job. You realise you are riddled with self-doubt; these thoughts are not helpful, and you realise they are mainly fear based, highly self-critical and not true. So as these thoughts inevitably pop up, you decide to acknowledge the thought but not engage in it. You move to create a distraction, perhaps with the task you are doing, or with a replacement positive thought (*Everyone is nervous on their first day, everyone starts off with lots to learn on the job, I can't get it all right straight away*).

3. If the thought is a *No thanks, I'll pass on this one*, then you do not engage with it and you move on to your next thought. Either your next thought will be there ready to go, or you find a distraction. Strangely, just acknowledging a thought is usually enough to have it move along (just like the 'dot' experiment). If your unwanted/unhealthy thought remains in front of you, however, then focus on something else. This needs to be something that keeps you busy and uses your brain, such as a brain puzzle game or tidying the cutlery draw – whatever works. Whatever comes to mind or is in front of you. The mind is like a television: if you change to another thought or focus, you have changed channels and the previous channel (or thought) is no longer playing. It is true that this unwanted/unhealthy thought can (and will) pop back up again. That is okay; it just means that you continue with this approach each time. When we choose not to engage with our thoughts and we do not fuel them, they become weaker over time. We also strengthen the mind's ability to concentrate and to be calm.

A FEW POINTERS

1. Take comfort; no one can control what pops into their heads – it is on random play. It's not just you. Everyone is in the same boat.

2. Great news! You can reprogramme your mind. When you keep engaging in a thought, the thought's neural pathway is fuelled, so the thought then plays more and more frequently. When you move away from engaging in a thought theme, you starve the neural pathway and it becomes weaker, so it comes to mind less often and it moves away from your 'favourites' list.

3. It is much more difficult to do traffic control on our thoughts when we are tired, stressed or feeling vulnerable. It takes more effort and self-discipline not to just go with it and jump into the downward spiral of unhealthy and unhelpful thinking. But ironically, this is when you will benefit the most. You are already in a bad spot, so it is that much more important to be in damage control and keep your head above water.

4. It takes time. When we kick our toe, it really hurts, so why do we not panic? Because while it is painful, we know it will soon pass. So too with unhealthy or unhelpful thoughts (and stressors while we are at it). When we find ourselves feeling a weight of negative thinking and acutely painful emotion, we need to focus on the fact that probably by tomorrow, we will have

moved through and past it (maybe in an hour – even five minutes!). Yes, the problem might still be there, but our intensity of thought and emotion will not be as acute; we will be in a different place. So keep an eye on the horizon, and take heart in the fact that you will move through and past where you are now. You will be okay. Maybe not immediately, but soon.

5. You cannot shut out thoughts. You can acknowledge and choose not to engage with thoughts, but you cannot just stop them or block them. If you try to block them, then they just become more powerful. It is like in martial arts, it is better to work with the opponent's movement towards you, and guide their force past you, than to block it and take the full force. This is how it works. If you try not to have a thought, you actually strengthen the thought because you have to access the thought to decide not to have it. For example, if you try not to think of a pink rabbit, you will have to think of a pink rabbit, before you can decide to *not* think of a pink rabbit. Strange, hey? So observe and deflect (distract), don't try to stop and block your thoughts.

6. You can quieten the traffic of thoughts by learning to choose whether to engage or not to engage in them, purely by not fuelling the unhelpful unhealthy thoughts. The other way to quieten your thoughts is to work through your issues and therefore create more peace of mind, and through regular mindfulness practice (Books 2 and 3). This does not stop the stream

of thoughts, of course; it just slows them down. A quieting of thoughts is more calming and peaceful, but crucially it means less effort is needed.

7. Once you get the hang of it, this choosing to engage or not in your thoughts becomes second nature. You can't unlearn knowledge, wisdom and skill. This all means less effort is needed as you become more of a pro at it. And you become curious to understand yourself and you enjoy your level of understanding. It makes you feel more confident and secure. There are lots of rewards for your efforts.

8. One of the major symptoms of anxiety and depression is self-absorption. The anxious and depressive person thinks about how they feel throughout their day. How they think and feel is an excessive focus. They ruminate, going around and around in circles with their anxious and depressive themes. They generalise their thoughts and feelings to other areas of their life and towards their future (that they feel degrees of hopelessness and helplessness about). This, of course, increases their depressed and anxious outlook and mood. While the goal is self-awareness and skill, it is actually about becoming extremely efficient with energy and concentration spent on our negative thoughts. This is quite the opposite of over-absorption and rumination. Our goal, ironically, is to become less self-focused (with regard to our thoughts and emotions) and get on to the good stuff

of living: finding meaning, making other people's lives richer, growing.

9. Life becomes more manageable. When thoughts come up and you are able to step back from them and see them clearly, then you will be able to prioritise. You will be better at making sensible decisions about what really needs your attention and what needs to be done. You will know when to take time out and self-care. When you recognise your thoughts as thoughts, this frees you from the distorted reality that these unhealthy and unhelpful thoughts create. This allows for more clear-sightedness and a greater sense of manageability in your life.

10. If we become impatient and think our old thinking patterns 'should' be able to change overnight, we are not only going to be disappointed, but we are discounting the strength of habit. We have probably taken years to develop our well-established thinking patterns, so it makes sense that it will take some time to translate new knowledge into new habits. On the way, however, we see progress and encouragement, as change is happening right before our eyes (between our ears!). This keeps us going and keeps our standards up as we reprogramme and take charge of our consciousness.

CHAPTER 25
HOW JUDGEMENTAL ARE WE!

When we start to observe our thoughts and work to control our consciousness, we become aware of our constant stream of judging and reacting to our inner and outer experiences. We have previously just been caught up in this and now we can learn to step back from it and see it. We constantly generate judgements about our experience and follow them with a lot of habitual behaviour. This is a whole separate area of growth, this opportunity to become aware of our automatic judgements. With this burst of self-awareness, we can start to see through our own prejudices and fears, and liberate ourselves to actually respond to situations and people with fact and proactive analysis of the situation, not blind reactive judgement and prejudice.

CHAPTER 26
DON'T BELIEVE EVERYTHING YOU THINK: IRRATIONAL BELIEFS

We know it is in our power to become healthier in our minds, but where do we begin?

The first step is knowing which of our beliefs warrant dispute. The second step is to debate and dispute our faulty thoughts in order to find truths, and not waste our time and energy on thoughts that are not accurate. This will be explored at lengths in the following sections. It is time to spring-clean our thoughts, to change the dialogue in our minds. We are now looking at improving the health of our thoughts, addressing our irrational beliefs. This is all about how we choose to respond to stressful situations. A statement that some believe came from Viktor Frankl, the Holocaust survivor I mentioned earlier, describes his own profound insights: 'Between stimulus and response there is a place. In that space is our power to choose our response. In our response lies our growth and our freedom.' Frankl illustrates that with awareness we all have freedom of choice in how to respond.

We often create our own limitations through our misperceptions. Practising mindfulness can help us break out of our ordinary patterns and wake us from automatic pilot mode. It can be hard to change thought and behaviour patterns due to this powerful force of conditioning. We tend to fall back into old habits because these are most familiar and habitual. Giving in to old habits means repeating negative patterns, which is a bit like banging our heads against the wall. It's not working and it's harmful to us, yet we continue to behave in our dysfunctional ways. We need to resist habitual reactions by turning off our autopilot. A necessary first step in order to increase our proactive choice is to become truly aware of the stresses in our life and how we respond to them.

CHAPTER 27
YOUR NEGATIVE SELF-TALK IS YOUR INFORMANT

Your negative self-talk is your informant – your guy on the inside.

The anxious loops that keep spinning in our heads as they exacerbate our fears are the areas that we want to make healthy. This negative self-talk flags the themes of our consciousness that are off track. These specific areas, our Achilles heels, are the areas where we need to learn to control our consciousness.

For example, if you regularly had the thought *I'm not good enough*, what might this say about your belief system? What about *Nobody understands me?* What are *your* negative self-talk themes? Consider the historical events that led you to these personal fear thoughts. It is usually a combination of experiences with our family, our friends, and our culture. It would be a valuable investment to spend a week recording your negative self-talk. This helps you study yourself and become an expert on your mind. Note the repetition, the themes, how the next day you might not agree with your distressing sureness the night before.

We have all developed deeply ingrained habitual styles of thinking that keep us stuck in a stress reaction, such as exaggerating negative thoughts or feelings, catastrophising and blaming. Throughout our lives, our thoughts have created our reality. What a wonderful thing that we can grab the reins and re-skill to change this level of conscious control and fundamentally change our experience of ourselves, others and our world.

CHAPTER 28
EXTREME NEGATIVE SELF-TALK

We go to extremes. All or nothing. Black and white.

The world teaches us to have constant self-doubt instead of loving our own worth. Our negative self-talk presses our buttons; we fear these statements, so they get traction and we think them, then believe them. The following are common negative self-talk themes that really cause damage to us and have zero validity. This is about knowing your demons, your fears, and knowing your Achilles heel. What negative self-talk comes to *your* mind during times of stress?

- I am worthless, no good, of no value

- Any person that offends me is a total #####

- I can't stand it, I can't cope, I'm going crazy

- I am coming to harm, I am sick, I am vulnerable

- Winning is everything; if I don't come first, I am a loser

- Beauty is everything; to be valued and liked, I must be physically attractive

- Things should be a fairytale/better than they are, the world should be perfect

- If I am alone, I am worthless and rejected

- I have no power or control in my life

- I am a victim of life; the world/fate is unfair and has done me wrong.

Whichever of these negative self-talk themes you experience, they become your 'hot issues' and vulnerable points. If we looked into your mind, I am sure we would find a broken record of recurring thoughts that shape how you see yourself and your world. You keep tripping up on them. What are they? We all need to get clear about what our most common and problem negative self-talk themes are.

CHAPTER 29
LEVELS OF CONSCIOUSNESS

Taking a moment to cover levels of consciousness is important because we need to understand and respect that we are not always aware of the cause of our stress response.

We have three levels of consciousness. Our **conscious awareness** is here and now: you are reading this book, aware of the room around you and aware of the thoughts and feelings you are currently experiencing. Our **subconscious awareness** involves the vague information that we don't grasp clearly. When we 'know we know, but we can't think what we know'. It's what we feel when we say, 'It's on the tip of my tongue' or 'Leave it with me and it will come to me'. I drive a manual car to work, but I couldn't tell you which foot goes on the clutch without almost role-playing the actions.

Then there's the **unconscious**: the great unknown. Our unconscious holds our archives of memories and primitive drives. We process things on a level beyond all awareness in our unconsciousness. The only time we can connect with our unconscious is when we dream (see Book 2, Chapter 28).

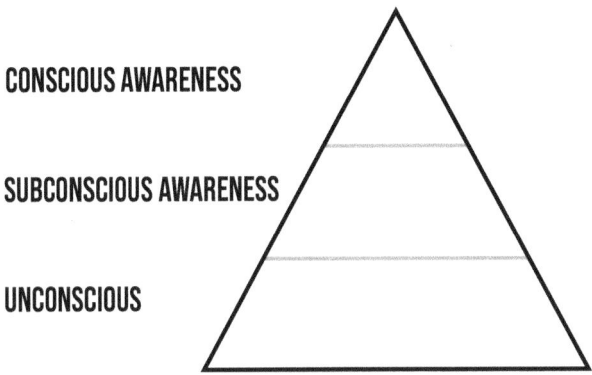

What is interesting is that we can experience stress on any of these three levels of consciousness. Of course, we can only explicitly work with our conscious awareness, and vaguely with our subconscious awareness. Our unconscious keeps us humbly clueless, as we don't have all of the information on what we are working with.

Being mindful of the role of our unconscious shows us that it is okay to be stressed and not know why. For example, our trigger for anxiety and panic attacks might come from an unconscious source, which can be very confusing. We can find it unsettling to concede that our behaviour is not always due to our conscious control. Instead, a large chunk of our behaviour is due to our unconscious mind and as such it is below our level of awareness. When we find ourselves repeating the same mistakes and destructive patterns of behaviours again and again without conscious intention, then our unconscious is tapping us on the shoulder and saying, 'Here I am, be open to learn and listen to me.' Try to follow the clues.

CHAPTER 30
YOUR DYSFUNCTIONAL STYLES OF THINKING

We need to do the headwork so we can work out what thoughts are true or not true (rational vs irrational), and are helpful or not helpful. This is where our habitual styles of thinking come in. We interpret events negatively and inaccurately, due to our dysfunctional patterns of thinking. We react to events unconsciously and so quickly that we don't notice we are doing it. So we just keep repeating our patterns of interpretation, and feeling physically tense, stressed, anxious, sad or angry. When we become aware of our patterns of dysfunctional thinking, we can catch ourselves and hold our thinking accountable. We can learn to become healthier if we practise choosing our interpretations. By just recognising these patterns and realising they are not accurate, the dysfunctional thinking pattern unravels, and we are left with the facts. We can ask ourselves, 'Is there another, healthier way that I can view this situation differently?'

THE BIG SEVEN: TYPES OF DYSFUNCTIONAL THINKING PATTERNS

1. **Mind reading** involves believing that you know what other people are thinking and feeling. We believe we know why others act the way they do. These beliefs are held with no actual evidence. We jump to conclusions. For example, we may incorrectly assume that our partner knows why we are upset, when they actually have no idea and are trying to guess. Or we assume that, because of their manner, someone is thinking negatively about us, when in fact they are just in a bad spot and have not paid special attention to our interaction. These interpretations lead us to think that someone doesn't like us or is out to get us. Such interpretations tend to cultivate anxiety and depression and can negatively impact relationships.

2. I am re-mentioning the **'shoulds'** because they are such a common problem that leads to guilt and resentment. This thought pattern involves having a list of absolute rules and judgements and imposing them on yourself and others. 'You should think to hang the washing out', 'I should keep up with my gym classes'. If we rephrase and talk about what we *want* ourselves and others to be doing and why, only then can we get some constructive power to help this issue along. Instead, say, 'What I *will* do' or 'What I *want* to do'.

3. **Catastrophising** is the cornerstone of anxiety. It is a style of thinking that blows the situation way out of proportion. We take one event and from it we automatically expect disaster and imagine the worst possible outcome. We go to extremes and create worst-case scenarios. For example, a parent might have a conflict with their teenager, and they have not handled it well. They think, *I'm a terrible parent, I can't get anything right, our relationship is ruined*, when they have actually only had one unhelpful interaction.

4. **Blaming** others involves getting the source of responsibility very wrong. We hold others responsible for our behaviour and our experiences when it is really our responsibility. There's always someone to blame. There is always something outside of ourselves to blame. Apart from not being accurate, the problem is that we can't change others and may not be able to change the circumstances; we can only change ourselves, and we are only fully responsible for ourselves. When we blame, we deprive ourselves of our choice, of our power to create change. Remember, it is all about choice and awareness.

5. **Being the eternal expert** is when we feel pressure to always be right. We cannot relax and be fallible, and just be open to learning. We are always on duty and defending the fact that we are always the resident expert. Apart from being extremely exhausting, this is simply impossible. We do not and cannot know

everything, and we don't need to. This dysfunctional thinking pattern is based on significant insecurities. Somewhere we have learnt that we are not good enough or that we will be judged and criticised if we are wrong. We feel that it's not safe to be vulnerable. We are overcompensating for feeling insecure, and feeling insecure about being insecure.

6. **Exaggerating the negative and discounting the positive** always work together to contribute to anxious and depressive moods. We downplay positive experiences so that they are not acknowledged, while magnifying and giving power to negative experiences so that they are way out of proportion. With a success we say, 'I just had good luck' or 'The competition wasn't great'; we somehow melt the positivity away from the positive. We disqualify other good things that we have achieved or experienced. With the negative, we may have a mishap in the morning, and we respond with, 'The day is ruined' or 'I'm going to have a bad day'. We overgeneralise a single event and see it as an *always*. Instead of a grey situation, we see black or white. We jump to conclusions, are quick to find a negative label such as 'I am a loser', and we exaggerate the importance of our own mistakes.

7. **Personalisation** is when we see ourselves as the cause of negative events that we are not fully responsible for. We are not looking at others' responsibility for themselves or contextual factors that shaped the

situation. It is usually more accurate that we may have only partly contributed to the problem.

We need to become aware of our dysfunctional thinking patterns, catch them as they happen, rein them in and hold them accountable with a healthy framework of rational thinking. If these dysfunctional thinking patterns are left to erode our experiences, we face anxiety, depressive mood and physical tension and stress. We gain insight when we step outside of our dysfunctional thinking patterns. We learn the inner workings of our mind. Instead of being controlled, we take control of our consciousness.

CHAPTER 31
FIGHT THE GOOD FIGHT; ARGUE WITH YOURSELF

Your thoughts have power. They create your world and shape your life.

We now need to rewrite the outdated thinking that drives you. Once we have identified our dysfunctional thoughts, the goal is to test them and to replace them with thoughts that are more functional and true. Have you noticed that with others you are very capable of being rational, balanced and compassionate in your feedback to them? You are much kinder to others than yourself; you are more able to soothe your loved ones. Why?

With others, we have distance from the problem so we can access our reasoning skills. We need to use our new ability to observe our thoughts; we need to know our dysfunctional patterns so we can analyse our thoughts more objectively. Each time we recognise a thought *as a thought*, and each time we ask ourselves how accurate it is and how strong its hold on us is, we are strengthening our mindfulness.

When we have grabbed a negative thought, we need to know how to argue with it. There are four skills to help pull our thoughts apart and hold them accountable. They are evidence, alternative causes, de-catastrophising and reprogramming our thoughts. These are summarised below.

EVIDENCE

When arguing with a negative belief we need to show that it is factually incorrect. Facts ground the issue and our overreactions. Put on your detective hat. What is the evidence for this belief? This is about facts; we are exposing the distortions in our thinking. Is it a catastrophe or is it a hurdle to work around? Reality is usually on your side. For example, you may have an argument with your partner. If you look at the evidence, you may see that this doesn't happen often. You acknowledge that you are both hurting. You both have different problems that need to be heard and addressed. You realise this conflict state will recover within a day or two and if there is good listening and learning you can strengthen as a couple from this and even be glad of the conflict in the end. This is an example of facts overcoming an original fear response.

ALTERNATIVES

What are *all* of the factors and variables that led to the situation you are having negative thoughts about? Most negative situations (for example, someone behaving inconsiderately, or feeling that you did not do well at a task) have many causes. When we are being dysfunctional in our thinking, we routinely focus on just one cause. This approach is not accurate because it is not comprehensive. This approach can also be negatively biased (looking at the worst in the situation) and is usually designed to undermine someone, whether yourself or others.

A healthy headspace and healthy interpretation has reality on its side. There are of course multiple causes to a problem situation, so we need to learn to look at the *whole*, not just a part. We need to look at *all* the factors, not just the damaging insidious explanations. To dispute our negative thinking and beliefs, we need to scan for all of the possible contributing causes. We then need to focus on those factors that are specific to that situation and avoid generalising to other times. This means trying to be as objective as possible and steering away from using our fears and insecurities to guide our reasoning. This is probably going to be extremely challenging because we are so familiar with being subjective and negatively biased. Healthy thinking will really stretch you. It takes skill and persistence to control your consciousness. Practise being proactive, not reactive.

DE-CATASTROPHISING

When there is a legitimate, fact-based, negative outcome or problem, we need to make sure that we implement the skill of de-catastrophising. This is about keeping the problem in proportion, remembering the countering positives, dropping the words 'always' or 'never', and remembering that we will recover with time. Like any other skill, this involves learning and practice. We need to practise grounding ourselves in reality and not letting ourselves spiral or blow the problem out of proportion. We need to search for evidence and really think of the implications. Ask yourself: is it a problem for now, for the short term, middle term or 'forever'? Is this one bad action just one part of your behaviour (or another's behaviour), or does it mean you (or they) are a bad person, doomed for eternity? Rather than thinking, *I screwed up the exam, it's all a disaster, I'm a failure*, we can learn to de-catastrophise and think, *This is one exam, and there are plenty of other things that I can do well. I can also do more preparation for the next exams to lift my results.*

REPROGRAMMING OUR THOUGHTS

One of the great things about being human is that we are able to learn. So let's stop repeating our dysfunctional thinking patterns and banging our head against the wall, and actually learn an alternative thinking pattern that helps us to be healthy.

A crucial approach is to examine ways you can change the situation in the future. Even if the belief is true now, how can you make changes to get a better outcome next time? For example, *I was very withdrawn at the party and did not engage much. I therefore did not have many people talk with me. It is not their responsibility to hold my hand and draw me into conversations at these things. Next time I will actively scan for someone I am drawn to and I will put in effort to find and build mutually interesting conversations. That is my challenge.* This is taking responsibility rather than indulging the dysfunctional thought of, *No one talked to me. I was a social failure; I can't do parties. I'm disgusting.*

> *We can have our worries,*
> *but we can choose not to worry about them.*
> Garry, thirty-nine-year-old client

When we face negative events in our daily life, we need to listen closely to our thoughts, beliefs and interpretations. We need to do mindful self-inquiry. The relief we feel, the sense of empowerment that comes, and our new ability to recover more quickly from hurdles – these are beautiful and life changing. By becoming grounded and healthy in our thinking patterns, we can go from feeling despairing and overwhelmed to feeling hopeful and purposeful.

When replacing thinking with healthy, constructive self-talk, please use positive comments and not double negative comments. Double negatives are when you say it is not a negative. Some examples are 'I'm not bad at cooking', 'She's not bad', 'He's not ugly'. Why we use double negative statements and not just positive statements, I do not know. The problem with double negatives is that the brain has to go to the negative statement, and then work to move away from it. We are just putting our focus on the negative statement. The positive intended message is not received. An example is the exercise I mentioned previously: 'Don't think of a pink rabbit'. We will think of a pink rabbit and then try to move away from this thought. It is the same with self-talk. It is crucial that we skip the habitual double negative thoughts, and we just use self-affirming positive statements in our daily involvement and love relationships. Instead of thinking something like, *I should not have asked her out, of course she rejected me, no one would want to be with me, I'll never find anyone*, an accurate approach is, *It's good I tried; it took courage and I can't not be in the ring. I'll wait till I click with someone. Of course, I will meet someone; it's a matter of who and when. I have to keep meeting people if I want to find someone, so I'm going to stay open to this.*

CHAPTER 32
OUR EMOTIONAL LAG

Old bad habits can't be blocked or erased. Unfortunately, that's not how the brain works. Our habits with our behaviour, our way of communicating and our defensive automatic reactions are a series of thoughts that are caused by neural pathways that are clumped together. The more you have used these neural pathways in the past, and the more detail that is added to these thinking patterns, the thicker the neural pathway clump gets.

To reverse this, you don't delete a bad habit (or a neural pathway clump); you build a new one. You build a better model. You fuel this new neural pathway over and over again, so that it grows and eventually this new habit is stronger than the old one. You then start to automatically go to the new stronger habit, rather than the old, now weaker one. When the new habit dominates the old unhealthy one, then our emotional experience turns on its head. Instead of us triggering our threat system with all of the negative emotions attached, we are triggering our comfort system, with soothing, positive emotions.

We can work through years of previous bad depressive and anxious habits in this way, one clump of dysfunctional neural pathways at a time. When we fuel and strengthen our comfort system, we feel contentment and inner calm. That is a clear reward for our determination and insight. The problem is that while we are wrangling with our previous dysfunctional thinking habits, our emotions are going to remain in threat response (fear, sadness and so on), until our new rational thinking habits take over.

Think of it this way: our emotions are a bit cheap, and can be bought by the biggest muscle. Our emotions hang out with whichever is our strongest thought pathway. When our old, toxic thinking has the most strength, our emotions will hang out with that way of thinking. When our new, healthy thinking gets stronger and becomes the biggest muscle, then our emotions will swap sides or alliances. Our thoughts join the healthy team and we then feel the positive, healthy emotions.

The key is to understand this and not get discouraged if we are not feeling any emotional relief immediately. We need to understand that while we are working away at replacing our dominant thinking pattern, we might continue to feel distressed by the issue. We have an emotional lag. This is normal and is to be expected, but can be really tough going. We need to persevere to eventually get our emotional rewards.

Our emotions will swap allegiance when a newer stronger neural pathway comes along.

Let's map out where emotions fit in. Our thoughts shape our emotions.

Positive thoughts = positive emotions.

Negative thoughts = negative emotions.

Our emotions can influence our thinking, but more often our thoughts shape our emotions. Emotions also shape behaviour. For example, they influence our decision about whether to go out and be bubbly in our social world or stay home and hide.

Thoughts also shape behaviours enormously. They are basically a green light or a red light for our behaviours – for example, whether we approach someone or not will be determined by whether we perceive them as friendly or a threat.

Behaviour also influences thoughts and emotions. When we go for a walk, our thoughts and emotions become more positive. If we stay cooped up in a dark room, our thoughts and emotions are probably going to deteriorate.

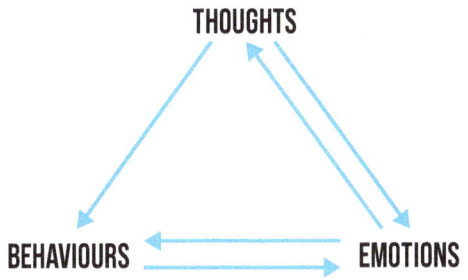

It is a skill to understand and respect our emotional lag. We start with a dysfunctional negative thought; our emotion is linked to this thought so we feel sad or perhaps afraid. We need to dispute this dysfunctional thought and work to change our approach to a healthy thought or belief. This is new to us, and the neural pathway that has been created is still weaker than our old dysfunctional thought pathway. We persist with staying rational, and practise, practise, practise. With time and persistence, this new functional way of thinking becomes the more dominant thinking pattern. We know when this happens because our emotions flip over and change teams to the now stronger (rational) positive thinking pattern/neural pathway. This is a very big breakthrough, and it feels great. It is an 'aha' moment. The 'penny drops'; we feel a lightness in our being; we feel a physical weight being lifted. This is when we feel a release from long-held stress, from the previous anchor that has held us underwater.

Here is a concrete example. When I drive in the US, it is a significant and daunting adjustment for me to go from driving on the left to driving on the right-hand side of the road. Driving on the right freaks me out at first. I start off scared; it feels very wrong. My emotions, fear and apprehension remain until, with practice, practice, practice driving on the right, this becomes my new normal (my new dominant neural pathway). Then the positive emotion of confidence follows. This is an example of learning a new healthy and adaptive thought and behaviour, with emotion following along in time. Emotion is always the last to catch up, and only comes after we have reprogrammed through practising new healthy habits of thinking or behaviour.

Negative thought

Negative thought triggers negative emotion

Practice replacing your negative thought with a more helpful positive thought. Your negative emotion will remain because your negative thought is still the more dominant thought.

Practice × 10, or × 20, or × 30?

New positive thought becomes the dominant thought (the new 'norm'). Triggers resulting reward of positive emotion.

CHAPTER 33
EMOTIONAL WILDERNESS

Our emotions are crucial to our human experience and provide us with information about what is going on within us. Let's skill up on emotions. Our negative emotions can include despair; we can feel as if we are drowning. We can feel incredibly volatile, as if we could crack at something as simple as a bird chirping. We can feel overwhelmed by everything. Our stressors can seem like enormous mountains or deep gullies. It can feel impossible to get around them.

By contrast, our positive emotions are the richness of connection with others, the belly laughter that makes us lose ourselves in bliss, the savouring of heart-warming experiences from a beautiful sunset to a friend's smile. We can feel a tenderness for the world and our loved ones; we can feel intrigue and passion, all the way to quiet contentment.

Emotions are very real, very strong and very powerful. When someone asks us, 'How are you?' we don't reply with a summary of our thoughts or our behaviours, we reply with a summary of our feelings. The barometer for how our day, our life, our relationships, our sense of self and our view of the future is rated is based on our feelings. Typically, emotions have a lot of control of us – usually more control then we have over our emotions.

Let's now work out the role of our feelings and how to work with them rather than have them work against us.

SMILE

Smiling is emotionally contagious within yourself. Research has found that when you are required to smile – when you are forced to tense your facial muscles around your eyes as in a smile – you actually start a neurological domino effect, activating your brain activity associated with positive emotion. How about that? Genuine smiling promotes a more positive mood, and *obliged fake smiling does also*. So smile more; you will feel better for it! Perhaps we should all go start working as greeters at department stores?

CHAPTER 34
EMOTIONS WASHING OVER YOU

If emotions are predominantly a *symptom* of thoughts and behaviour, what do we do with them?

In truth you don't have a choice, because you can 'run but you can't hide' from your emotions. If you put up a dam wall then the pressure just builds, and this can cause more problems and pain for you. Some people are very skilled at processing their emotions and managing them, while others are very unskilled. Let's make sure you are in the skilled group to help you become emotionally buoyant.

First you need to acknowledge the feelings you're directly experiencing, without trying to censor them. It's not useful to shut them down with an 'I'm fine!' This is about being real with our emotions. Learning to 'go with it' rather than fighting it allows the pain to change and often diminish. This means acknowledging whatever you feel, and letting the waves of emotions and sensations go over you. This means just sitting with your anxiety, your sadness, your emotion. Experience your emotion with curiosity and just see what happens.

It does *not* mean diving in and swimming around in our emotions. The goal is not to whip them up and make them grow. It is instead about taking responsibility for our emotions and observing them. The emotions do not drown you. By acknowledging emotions and letting them go, they can wash over you and then leave. The emotions won't hurt you; they can be really unpleasant, but they won't cause damage to you. Your emotions are not dangerous; they can only help you in becoming an expert on yourself.

It's as if you're becoming familiar with your emotions so that you are no longer afraid of them. You let the sadness inside and then you say to yourself, 'All right, it's just sadness. I don't have to let it control me. I see it for what it is.' When you feel fear or loneliness, you let go and let the tears come. Feel it completely, but then say, 'All right, that was my moment with fear or loneliness; now I'm going to put those feelings aside and change to a different emotion'. It is about not being afraid of our feelings, but rather, when it is a convenient moment, pouring them out and releasing them. There is a time to acknowledge an emotion, feel the emotion, and then let it go. This is learning the skill of observing your emotions and not being dragged along or defined by them. We learn to tell ourselves, 'That's fear. I'm going to separate from it and walk away from it now.'

Learn the skill of observing your emotions and not being dragged along or defined by them.

Recognising our emotions does not mean that we agree with our emotions and are okay or at peace with them. You will have many emotions that you do not agree with and you wish you could deny and avoid. But the emotions are there, and you have to release them. For example, if we feel envy when we see a positive in others, we are not proud of this, yet due to our headspace, here we are. You still have to recognise this envy, let it wash over you and leave you.

We can learn so much from our emotions. When we study them, especially the ones we are not proud of, we can work backwards and study the thoughts that have led us to these emotions. For example, negative thoughts and insecurities about ourselves may lead us to behave in a less than generous way towards someone we perceive as more accomplished than us … and then we feel envy *and* guilt at the same time. This is information that is helpful to know. We can go back to the source – our negative thoughts and insecurities – and work them out more. We aim to fix the problem and not just continue to mop up the consequences or repeat the problem. Another positive is that we keep getting better at recognising our emotions and their origins. With more skill we have more information and more control of our consciousness.

It is not easy to acknowledge and feel difficult emotions. When we face anxiety, stress, or emotional pain it may seem unsafe, and we may feel unwilling. It can also feel a bit foreign since our culture often tells us to suppress, deny and shut down our emotions. This is not only for negative emotions, but positive emotions also. How often do we feel a surge of positive emotion, but we cap it because we fear that others will not share our experience? We want to go under the radar. Of course, there is the pressure not to cry, not to be vulnerable. But we are all vulnerable. And if you are human you feel painful emotions. What is the point of denying the obvious? We need to learn to view our emotions as challenges, as rites of passage to being a healthy adult, instead of running away from them. It is then that we can learn and grow. It is only then that we can change the causes of negative emotions and change our thinking pathways to a healthier direction.

We are all vulnerable.

When you learn to go with what's happening rather than fighting it, suffering and resistance often lessen. It is an amazing piece of wisdom to know that difficult emotions and associated physical sensations (like an anxious stomach) do indeed pass. To trust that we will move on to another emotion and we will be okay. We will soon be feeling like our old selves and enjoying some of the many positive emotions that are part of our world. This transient quality of difficult emotions gives us courage to acknowledge them and let them wash over us as we know they will soon end.

What to do? Throughout the next hour, day, week, month, bring recognition to any strong emotion and allow it to be present. Investigate what you feel and see where it takes you. Learn to understand that emotions are just another passing state of being and not a definition of who you are. Do not deny your humanness.

CHAPTER 35
WISDOM: THE COMMITMENT OF INTELLIGENCE, EMOTION AND WILL

Why is it that after thousands of years we have not figured all of this out? Why are we still so hopeless at controlling our consciousness and becoming free of society's pressures?

The main reason is that we must learn this kind of knowledge through experience, just as a craftsman needs to practise his skills. It is not a case of just memorising the ingredients and then being set for life. Control over consciousness is not simply a cognitive skill; it requires the use of your intelligence and willpower. Just like musicians and athletes, we need to keep *practising* what we know in theory. It is not just enough to *know* how to do it. And as we practise, the benefits gradually come to us. It is not a quick fix. We are building a life well lived, and we can take pride in crafting this over time. While it takes time to modify our habits of thinking and feeling, and we may need to wait for the new healthy habits to become our norm, at least we are feeling purposeful and empowered in our approach to living. While we wait for all the benefits to work, we are improving on our previous approach of being dragged through life on autopilot.

Those who take the trouble to gain mastery over what happens in their consciousness live a happier life.

This wisdom involves the constant questioning of where you are. And when you stop wanting to know, you're not living. You're sleepwalking again; you're on autopilot. Wisdom is not an answer. Wisdom is a question.

CHAPTER 36
PANIC: FIGHT / FLIGHT / FREEZE / FAINT

There are threats to our physical safety and there are threats to our psychological safety. We need to understand that our bodies do not differentiate between the two. But there is a serious twist: we accept one type of stress reaction, but freak out about the other. And it is this freak-out that can spiral into a panic attack.

I'll explain. What do we do if we are approached by an oncoming car, a lurking stranger or, as in our ancestor's days, a sabre-toothed tiger? We panic! Our heart races, our breathing is shallow and fast, our mind is racing with catastrophe. Extreme anxiety manifests itself physically. It can even feel like we are having a heart attack. Our bodies respond to this stress with an adrenaline rush (where neurotransmitters such as epinephrine and norepinephrine are released). What is interesting is that when there is a threat to our physical safety, we don't usually stop to notice our body's reaction. Our body's reaction to the physical danger just makes sense to us; it doesn't scare us. We are too busy thinking about the physical danger coming towards us.

But what if it is a psychological danger that we face? What if the threat is that someone might be breaking up with us, or that we have to speak in front of others and we fear we might screw up? Or that we feel others are being critical of us, or a loved one has a bad diagnosis, or we might not be able to pull off our business meeting? I could go on and on. These are examples of psychological threats: times when we don't feel psychologically safe. And, to be clear, this is our *perception* of our situation, not the actual situation. We may be perfectly safe and capable, but we do not perceive it that way; we perceive that we are in psychological danger.

Throw in here our phobias (like fear of flying) or obsessive-compulsive disorders (like not being able to check that the light switch is off), which are also psychological threats. How do we react? At the mild end, we feel tension and stress in our thinking, feelings and bodies. At the more severe end, we feel the same panic as if it is a physical threat like the sabre-toothed tiger.

Don't freak out about your body freaking out.

Our brains cannot tell the difference between physical and psychological threats, and our bodies react the same way for each. We experience the same fight, flight, faint or freeze responses. We experience the panic. But when we experience panic sensations from a psychological threat it does not make sense to us; it confuses us. We don't understand what is happening and we feel out of control. We can then even panic about panicking, which makes it spiral out further. In contrast, if we are in a car accident, we *expect* our heart to race and our breathing to become fast and shallow. But if we are going for a job interview, we also feel our heart racing and our breathing becoming fast and shallow, and this worries us. We think there is something strange happening and feel as if there is something wrong with our bodies.

Many poor souls experience panic attacks severely and frequently, and *this* makes them fear having *more* panic attacks. This is when it can evolve into a disorder. But let's be clear: experiencing panic is a natural human condition, and the sooner we understand what is happening to us and demystify it, the sooner we can calm ourselves and defuse our panic symptoms.

Unfortunately, there is another very important layer of complexity. Remember our levels of conscious awareness in Chapter 29? Our perceived psychological threats can come from any of these three levels of consciousness.

We may be *consciously* aware of a stressor – for example, if we walk into a party with unfamiliar people – or we might only have *subconscious* awareness, which might feel like a vague sense of apprehension that can't be pinned down. Or we may be completely *unconscious* of the stressor.

We really have no clue of what is going on within our unconscious selves. Unless we are primed by a dream in which we get a glimpse of our deeper workings, we really do not know what the themes of our unconscious are. As most of our internal information is in fact unconscious, it is extremely common for people to experience panic attacks with no conscious awareness of what they were stressed about. Without warning, their bodies appear to respond in a random fashion. As far as they are aware, they are okay and may even be feeling happy at the time. Then, *boom!* Panic builds up out of the blue. It can be really shocking to feel panic for no apparent reason. This type of panic happens when a person's unconscious is for some reason primed by stress to jump into this threatened response.

This kind of panic response happens when our conscious or unconscious thoughts trigger the ancient threat mechanism of fight, flight, freeze or faint, and we succumb to this response. We believe that something truly dangerous and fearful is happening to us. While in our modern world, these fight, flight, freeze and faint responses are usually just unpleasant and inconvenient, each of these is understood to have helped our ancestors.

- Fight: we would fight off the sabre-toothed tiger

- Flight: we would run like hell and climb a tree

- Freeze: we would stand frozen like a statue and hope the sabre-toothed tiger doesn't see us, or perhaps the beast will be attracted by someone who is running! Hope they go for the fresh meat.

- Faint: we would play dead and hope that the sabre-toothed tiger chases someone who is running – again, fresh meat!

… it's not looking good for the guy who is running!

We have the primitive part of our brain (old/reptilian/primal brain), and the higher order, executive thinking part of our brain (new/high order brain). While our primitive brain was inherited from our ancestors, our executive brain has been refined over time. We have been developing our executive brain to help us with decision making, rationalising, planning, reasoning, and learning.

The primitive brain takes in information from our senses and is all about perceiving danger. The key player is our **amygdala**, which activates our stress response and is responsible for releasing our stress hormones adrenaline and cortisol. We react to the threat with fast action. The amygdala cannot tell between physical or psychological threats, or real or imagined threats; it just gets triggered by our general perception of threat. So, whether it is an oncoming car or our excessive worrying about a future event, our bodies go through the same response. We may experience a few or all of these bodily reactions:

- Our breathing turns rapid as we are trying to get oxygen to our muscles for fight or flight. So we feel tight in our chest.

- When we don't fight or flee, this oxygen builds up, which causes us to feel dizzy.

- Our heart beats faster, as we are working hard to get oxygen around our body. We can feel as if our heart is going to fail. We can feel it beat through our chest.

- Our pupils dilate to allow us improved vision to judge our threat and our exit options. So our close-up vision becomes blurred.

- Our muscles tense as more blood is pushed to major muscle groups as we prepare for fight or flight. This makes our blood go away from our extremities, making our hands and feet feel clammy.

- We sweat to prevent our bodies overheating.

- Our blood pressure increases.

- We do not want to use our precious energy on our digestive system, because all oxygen and functioning focus needs to go to our muscles and limbs. Therefore, we have a feeling of needing to empty our digestive system; when we are anxious, we can feel like we want to vomit, or rush to the toilet with diarrhoea.

Perhaps our ancestors did quickly vomit or empty their bowels before they took on the sabre-toothed tiger. These days we very rarely vomit or have diarrhoea; we just have the horrible feeling that we are going to. We call it an 'anxious tummy' when anxiety causes us to feel sick in our stomachs from this threat response.

While this is the typical list of physical panic symptoms, we do have our unique patterns, and it is good to learn what our own sequence is. For example, on a milder level, we may recognise that a nauseous stomach ('anxious tummy') and tension around our shoulder blades, shoulders and neck are our early signs of stress, so we can work to defuse our pressure situation.

It causes problems when we misinterpret these anxious symptoms. Instead of viewing them as our understandable biological responses, we interpret them as actual evidence that the threat is real – that we are in danger. Sometimes we interpret this as if a catastrophe is imminent. It helps to know that anxiety attacks are a misinterpretation of our physical reactions. *We get anxious about being anxious.* We fear our heart racing, we fear feeling faint, we fear that we will vomit, we fear feeling out of control in public or at home. We fear the uncertainty and confusion of all these panic symptoms.

Despite millenia of evolution, we continue to experience these four panic responses today. You cannot choose your response. It happens automatically. It takes over your body suddenly. However, our life experience and level of confidence do influence which response will become automatically triggered within us. We tend to notice that we follow our own personal patterns. For example, I have noticed that when I feel danger I freeze, I struggle to speak up for myself and seem to be in shock (though I'm getting better at this!). But when a loved one or a stranger is in an emergency situation, I am wonderful; I barge in and take the crisis in hand with absolute confidence (that's fight mode kicking in).

An example of freeze is a man who walked in on his wife and his best friend having sex. His response? He froze; he stood in the doorway and could not say or do a thing. All he could do was walk backwards out of the room. They didn't even know he had caught them. He was frozen. Inside there were many things he wanted to do, but his body would not allow him. When someone is a victim of sexual assault, it is not uncommon to respond with freezing.

The best example of faint that I have come across is a couple of English-speaking eighteen-year-old girls who set off on their travels together. They chose a location to begin their adventure that was not very safe and where they could not speak the language. From their airport, they took a taxi. The taxi then drove in the opposite direction of their destination. One girl responded with fight; she yelled and protested ferociously. The other girl just fainted. She later woke up to see that the taxi driver had simply driven to another car to change vehicles as his car could not make the trip. Confronting first travel experience for the girls.

Interestingly and tragically, in a group, we humans tend to 'freeze'; we see a stranger in crisis and think that someone else will fix it or that it is not our place to fix it. We defer responsibility to others and don't presume it is our place to get involved. The person often gets no help from those in the crowd, who pass by or even stand watching, feeling mortified and pitiful in their frozen state. I have experienced this situation several times. Fortunately in these situations I have a 'fight' response and I get involved and become instrumental. I have come across a baby not breathing, with a group of fifty-odd people standing around frozen and terrified (I thought it was a group standing around street entertainment as I approached), and a few occasions of someone having a seizure in public. Happy to say everyone survived.

There is a difference between an anxiety attack and a panic attack. An **anxiety attack** involves all of those physical symptoms listed. A **panic attack** is when you have the same physical symptoms but you misinterpret what is happening and you catastrophise; you think you are going to die (usually believing that it is a heart attack). We are routinely using the phrase 'panic attack' here, however, because that is the common language used by the public.

Panic is safe.

And here is the big punchline. You do not die from a panic attack. Of course, if it brings on a secondary issue like asthma this can be very serious, but panic alone is not actually dangerous to your health. We only think and feel it to be dangerous to us. This is mainly because we feel out of control, and we humans hate being out of control. If we don't calm ourselves down, our bodies are designed to actually escalate our panic to the point where we faint. We then wake up when our bodies have rebooted, and we feel calm again – exhausted, but physically calm. While we are fainting, we actually swoon and have time to sit down, pull the car over, remove ourselves. Panic is a building of the storm within; it is not a sudden earthquake event. We are designed to have some time to calm it down or find a safe place to take time out.

Fainting, by the way, is actually pretty rare. Most often the panic symptoms just continue to harass us, but it is good to know that although panic attacks make us feel as if we are in physical danger, we are actually safe. As this is a very real part of being human, it makes loads of sense to know how to deal with this wild person within all of us. This is covered in Chapter 39 of this book, where we look at turning the panic off.

HELPING PANICKED OTHERS

When our loved ones are having a panic attack, we need to learn from them whether they want us to give them space or be there alongside them. We can help them to find a safe space. Realise that during a panic attack, your loved one is feeling that they are trapped, that they need to escape. Help them to find a space and feel safe, in order to relieve that feeling.

Know that with time the panic attack will run its course. Just be there and be calm. Be stable for them. Remind them that it will pass. Stay in the constant background even if they isolate themselves. Don't look for encouragement that you are doing the right thing; they are too consumed by their experience to engage with you. They are spinning out of control, and you are their rock, their anchor. Your calmness will be in stark contrast to their lack of control. Your loved one will eventually feed off your calmness and then be able to become calm themselves. They need to know someone cares. It is okay if you don't understand it; your willingness to help is what you need to offer. Your loved one needs to feel emotionally held.

SELF CARE WITH YOUR PANIC

If you tend to have a highly sensitive threat response or you have started to have panic attacks, then there is no room for self-criticism. This is unfair to you and only creates more pressure. This is a time for self-compassion, for getting alongside yourself and, with loving kindness and a gentle self-supporting hand, guiding yourself to becoming skilled in defusing your anxious threat response.

Just as someone with asthma needs to strengthen their lung capacity, if you are inclined to have a panic response, you need to become very strong and capable in this area. This is a reason to step up and attack the problem head on. You need to take control of your anxiety.

CHAPTER 37
OUR AUTONOMIC NERVOUS SYSTEM

This is a more in-depth run through of the anatomy of panic for your reference.

Our body is constantly assessing whether we are safe or not. Our **autonomic nervous system** guides how we respond to this assessment. It is part of the nervous system that controls involuntary functions. It is our automatic pilot; we have no vote on how it is activated. It is made up of two parts, or two neural pathways: the **sympathetic nervous system** and the **parasympathetic nervous system**. They complement each other. One is active in threat mode, the other is active in relax mode.

You can think of the sympathetic nervous system as the one that is in 'sympathy' with danger; it is our threat system. This is our go, urgent, launch mode. When our brain decides there is danger – physical danger or psychological danger – our brain activates our sympathetic nervous system. With this mode, our brain makes our breathing become shallow, our heart rate and blood pressure increase, and our internal immune, digestive and reproductive systems go 'on hold' as they are not useful when facing danger. We also have a surge of the brain chemicals (neurotransmitters) called **endorphins** which reduce our experience of pain. When our sympathetic nervous system is active, we can have a mild superhero moment – we can run further, be stronger and do physical feats that we normally cannot do. We are designed to really fight off that sabre-toothed tiger to the absolute best of our abilities – or rather, our enhanced abilities.

But we can't stay in this state. Firstly, often there is no physical danger to warrant using our enhanced mode – it could be a psychological danger we are facing. It is just our perception of the situation or our insecurities talking ('I can't do this'), and we find ourselves all wired and worked up with no use for our frenzied physical state. Yes, this is then a possible starting point for a panic attack. And even if there *is* a physical threat and sympathetic 'hyper' mode is appropriate, we can only stay in this state for a short time. Our resources run out, we become exhausted, or we just want to calm ourselves down. We also *need* to calm down so we can go back to looking for other threats in our environment. We cannot scan calmly for threat while we're being controlled by our sympathetic nervous system.

We need a balancer and a peacemaker. That is the role of our parasympathetic nervous system – our comfort system.

When we do routinely live in a constant state of stress, and function too long in our sympathetic nervous system, our body does not get a chance to rebalance itself. The effects can be severe and dangerous. Our immune system becomes suppressed, which means we have a reduced ability to fight disease. We can experience muscle tension, anxiety, migraines, high blood pressure (with all its complications), insomnia, and increasingly common gastrointestinal and digestive complaints (prolonged stress is a common cause of irritable bowel syndrome). The list is long. We can end up very unwell, with our quality of life psychologically and physically deteriorated.

We can rebalance our body by learning how to activate our parasympathetic nervous system and keeping it activated. This process returns us to a relaxed state. This is where our skills in breathing and mindfulness come in. We can learn to calm our perception of the psychological stress, and to bring our breathing and heart rate down. We can dramatically speed up the return to our parasympathetic nervous system. Swiftly jumping in and caring for ourselves is the key. You can think of it as self-care, parenting yourself, loving yourself, or regulating your thoughts and emotions.

CHAPTER 38
MIND-BODY CONNECTION

There is a significant link between mindfulness and stress reduction. This is an example of mind-body connection. Neuroscientists are launching into research to map out this connection, with exciting results. Neuroscience has proven that thoughts and emotions are interconnected, through neural pathways, with the functioning of our physical bodies. Mindfulness is the skilling up and mastering of these thoughts and emotions. We can shape our physical functioning through our control of our consciousness.

> In truth, our mind and body are the same thing.

The next section (Chapter 39) is the 'how to'; it looks at how to use the mind to soothe the body. It is essential to know how to steer your body. If you want to drive a car, you have to learn how to drive it. This is all about learning how to drive your body.

While we all need to learn these skills, it is really important to emphasise our *attitude* here. If you have a child in your care and your child panics, you as the adult step in and make sure you use a soothing but firm tone. It is in this way that you really need to take charge and parent and soothe *yourself*. Yes, this is difficult, but with awareness, skills, practice, experience and strengthening confidence, it becomes doable. You have to learn to not freak out about your body freaking out. You need to understand what is happening, know that it feels horrible and scary, but that you are safe. You then need to be sensible and work to calm yourself down. Ninety percent of the challenge is controlling your reaction. If you panic about panicking, your panic symptoms will just escalate and persist. With a matter-of-fact, aware, proactive response, you can calm your body's panic with speed.

CHAPTER 39
FORMAL MINDFULNESS PRACTICE

Drumroll – this is the exciting bit! This is where we bring psychological muscle to the table. If you have a vulnerability or a tendency towards anxiety or depressive mood, then daily meditation is non-negotiable. It is essential for you. If you have a tyre on your car that has a tendency to deflate, then you need ready access to an air pump. Formal mindfulness practice is your air pump. It is your best friend; it allows you to strengthen and become afloat in life, rather than drowning or being dragged along by your depression and anxiety.

When we talk about meditation, we are talking about formal mindfulness techniques. The two phrases are interchangeable. As discussed in Chapter 7, mindfulness can also be practised informally. Informal mindfulness is the skill of being *aware* in our moment-to-moment living as part of our lifestyle; it means doing things like being completely attentive while taking a bite of an apple, and taking note of the taste and texture – all the sensations. *Formal* practice involves taking the time each day to intentionally practise training your brain to concentrate, calm itself and connect with your body, thoughts, emotions and environment in the moment.

Anxiety and depression are about our thoughts – our bombardment of constant thoughts. Mindfulness practice quietens our thoughts; it stills our mind. It is about creating quietness in our minds. By engineering more quiet during our mindfulness practice, this quietness then spreads to our day-to-day lives. The traffic of thoughts learns to slow during our meditation, then the traffic learns to slow during the rest of our day. Gradually, you will notice the calmness spreading out. It is a slow, trickling-out effect. We are creating the relaxation response.

While we need to be patient here, we can feel the improvement and be encouraged as this calming of our mental muscle extends. We need to incorporate meditation as an essential in self-care in life, just like cleaning our teeth and eating. One of the great things about meditation is that you have it with you at all times. No equipment is needed, no one else is necessary and it's free. You can do it anywhere that suits you, anytime.

> Formal mindfulness = Meditation.
> Meditation = Formal mindfulness.

I want to skill you up so that you have the information and the options to practise formal mindfulness techniques and to reap the profound benefits. The information and the actual skills are straightforward and simple. The difficulty lies in building up our concentration skills and being prepared to actually *do it* and become more aware of ourselves, our thoughts, our feelings and our bodies.

WHY DO IT?

We do formal mindfulness practice because we want to stop living in a fog of racing thoughts, automatic reactions, and lack of awareness of ourselves and our potential. Formal mindfulness practice can not only bring greater balance to your mind, but it can actually create psychological and physical healing. We also use these mindfulness techniques to halt panic symptoms and return to our parasympathetic nervous system. It is wonderful to be able to get the most from your life – to radiate peace and stillness and to reduce suffering. It is wonderful to lessen problems like chronic stress disorders (psychological and physical), pain conditions and illness.

> Radiate peace and stillness in the room, watch how it changes the energy in a highly charged room.

Mindfulness doesn't just come about by itself. We can cultivate greater mindfulness through regular systematic, formal and informal mindfulness practice. We can make a huge difference to our health, balance and perspective from taking time out of the normal wear and tear of our 24/7 culture. Through mindfulness, we learn to cope with the constant and mounting stress from our multitasking and connectivity with the fast-paced world around us. We are taking a moment to remember who we are.

We tend to have little awareness of the relentless activity of our minds – how reactive and how driven we are by our incessant thoughts. This is because we do not routinely take time out to stop and observe our mind directly to see what it's up to. After becoming more self-aware of our inner processes, and understanding that they are passing mind states, we can apply these skills in our day-to-day lives. Through practising mindfulness you learn to be the observer of yourself, your reactions and your issues, rather than being inside them and just reacting. This is an inner strength and self-knowledge that is true wisdom. It is perhaps the ultimate human skill.

This inner stillness, patience and clarity takes you through all of your activities, pressure and busyness without taking stress on board. It then becomes normal not to be racing future-mindedly through experience, or spending your time ruminating and dwelling on the past. You are here *now*. The many forms of Eastern practice of meditation work to slow down the mind and reduce anxiety and be attentive to the present. This great tradition of Buddhism, the founder of mindfulness, focuses on achieving this serene state of mind.

The wisdom of mindfulness has reached beyond its Eastern origin, through psychology and into the medical science world. Physicians now understand the profound benefit of mindfulness and routinely prescribe this practice to help people reduce their stress, illness and pain. The important role of mindfulness is now also being appreciated and harnessed in neuroscience, education and the world of business. We are waking up to how humans work and how to create mental stability and capacity.

THE FORMAL MINDFULNESS TECHNIQUES: STOPPING PANIC

Let's sort out panic attacks first.

There are three steps or options in stopping panic in its tracks:

1. Understand what is happening, know you are safe and don't panic about panic. When we can redirect our brain to understand that we are not in fact in danger, we redirect and defuse our autonomic nervous system response. So basically, we need to call off the artillery. We are okay. We are just experiencing some uncomfortable physical symptoms, which include shallow breathing and rapid heart rate. We might feel as if an elephant is sitting on our chest. Even try to be bored with what your body is doing – then you will reverse your body's response.

2. If you can catch it early enough, distract yourself with something else that requires some brain power. Play a game on your phone, reorganise a cupboard, read a book. Passively watching a show won't cut it as you are not 'doing' or interacting with the activity. Just like changing the channel on your TV, change the channel of your mind. If we are distracted elsewhere and not engaged in the danger thought, our body stops responding to that danger thought. This is pretty hard to do, however, if the panic has had time to escalate and has become a tsunami.

3. Practise formal mindfulness. Learn to return speedily to your parasympathetic nervous system. To turn panic off we use *breathing techniques*. The breathing techniques work because they focus on exhaling, and it is the process of exhaling thoroughly that rebalances the body and calms the heart rate. Read below for some examples of formal mindfulness practices.

After you have defused your panic response, prepare to feel exhausted, as if you have run a psychological marathon. Sleep it off and you will recover.

MINDFUL BREATHING: YOUR BEST FRIEND

Mindful breathing is a cornerstone of mindfulness and is the treatment intervention for panic attacks as it regulates the stress response and slows the heart rate. These breathing techniques communicate to our body that we are safe, and that everything is okay.

While it is nice to do mindful breathing in a relaxing environment without distractions, it is versatile. When you are stressed and even when you're not, you can actually do it anywhere, any time, and no one will know. You cannot, however, do it when you are speaking or eating, and I would advise not to do it while you are driving as it could reduce your concentration. Of course, if you are overcoming an onset of panic and you are working to pull the car over, mindfully breathe away!

Mindful breathing brings some structure and rhythm to your breathing. It involves thoroughly exhaling. Exhaling is the key to relaxation and gliding back to your parasympathetic nervous system. When we are stressed, we tend to inhale and not exhale enough. Think of the old breathing into the paper bag technique. This was about focusing on filling the paper bag – exhaling!

> Exhaling is the key to relaxation.

Breathing techniques take our focus away from our head and bring it to our body. They slow down our brain activity and invite in our comfort system. By taking slow deep breaths we release anti-stress enzymes and calming hormones. This is about changing our pattern of breathing – our breath rate and depth.

If you are new to deep breathing, be gentle and patient with it. You may need to build up your practice slowly. As you continue, you will be able to breathe in and breathe out mindfully for more counts. Start with a couple of minutes, and then gradually extend to doing the breathing techniques for longer.

The following are techniques for you to play with and choose what fits for you. You can do these with your eyes shut if you feel comfortable; this can allow you to really focus. If you feel more comfortable with your eyes open, then just look in one direction to reduce your visual traffic.

Important:
Your intention is for you to keep your mind on the breath. Notice when you get distracted away from your breathing by a thought. Without judgement or beating yourself up, just let the thought go and return your attention lightly to the breath.

Breathe through your nose if you can, or your mouth if you need to.

SOME BREATHING TECHNIQUES

1. Breathe out for a count of 10

I'm going to list this breathing technique first as perhaps it is the primary breathing technique; I recommend it to clients for panic attacks (although of course they can also choose any technique from those listed below). It is very thorough, and it encourages the improvement and the advancement of this skill.

It is extremely simple.

Breathing with your belly (abdominal breathing) can be helpful in overcoming anxiety and stress. If your breathing is irregular or shallow, this can help to settle it. With shallow breathing, we use our upper lungs and let our shoulders rise. Instead, we want to use our diaphragm. Our diaphragm is like an elastic band that reaches from one of our sides to the other; when the elastic band goes down towards the ground, it expands the lower lungs, giving us a lovely deep breath. If our stomach goes out as we breathe in, it means that we are using our diaphragm and our lower lungs. This is why we promote 'belly breathing'.

Put your hand on your belly and slowly breathe in. Feel your belly expanding as you inhale.

So, gently belly breathe in. Then breathe out gently, while in your head you are counting 1 through to 7. Remember:

slow, slow, slow. Try to keep the pace slow and the rhythm of your counting regular. If you find you can manage it, extend to breathing out to a count of 8, then 9, then 10. The goal is to tone your diaphragm so that you can comfortably and slowly breathe out to a count of 10. Singers and musicians who use wind instruments will probably nail this as they have toned diaphragms. When you practise this, you become really comfortable and natural with it.

2. Just notice your breath

As discussed earlier, this is simply noticing and being mindful as you breathe in and out. You do not need to change your breathing or do anything. You could notice whether you are choosing to use your mouth or your nose and notice the feelings of the air moving past your skin through your nostrils or your lips. There is a whole level of intricate information here that we usually have no awareness of. You can notice your belly or your chest moving in and out.

3. Box breathing

Box breathing is for all of you visual people, and it's wonderful for children. The key is to keep the pace nice and slow. You can visualise this. Breathe in as you imagine scanning with your eyes along the first then the second side of a box. Then hold your breath for five seconds, then breathe out as you scan your eyes along the third and fourth sides. Again pause your breath for five seconds. And repeat.

Another option is to allow someone to help you. Have a loved one trace the outline of this large square on your back or arm with their finger. If you are doing this with your child and helping them to do their breathing exercise, you can gently trace the image on their skin, and they can follow along. The added bonus of course is they may find the touch calming.

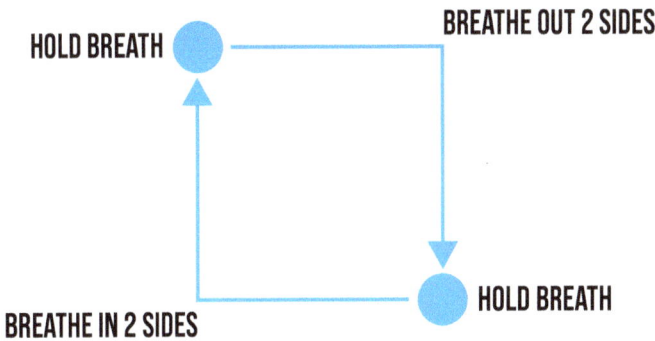

Alternatively, you can think of the same concept with just counting and without visualising the box. Breathe in for a count of 4, hold for 2, breathe out for a count of 4, hold for 2 and continue. It really depends on your preference.

4. Candle fingers

This was perhaps designed for children, but I have many adult clients who prefer it as it is so visual and sensory, and it forces you to keep an even tempo in your exhaling. This is excellent and grounding for when you are losing your head with panic.

Basically, put your hands out and fingertips out, palms facing you. You gently blow out onto each of your ten fingertips: 1, 2, 3 … 9, 10, as if they were candles to blow out. This makes you pace yourself and exhale thoroughly. It also takes some of your concentration from your stressor. It's lovely.

5. Blow on a candle

This is popular with teenagers. Light a candle. Your job is to blow on the flame very gently, slowly and gradually, while making sure you do not blow the flame out. The gentleness of this is what helps us again to exhale slowly and perhaps thoroughly. It gets us to control our breathing, and again it is a task that can distract us from our stressor. A flame can also be pleasantly hypnotic if you focus on it.

6. Walking in breath

We can use our body's natural movement to regulate our breath and our stress response. As we walk, breathe in for a count of four steps, and then breathe out for a count of six steps. Change it to a counting number pattern that works for you. The goal is to spend more time breathing out than breathing in. This is also a lovely way to help us stay focused. Before you know it, you will be focused on this calming rhythmic practice.

When we practise these breathing techniques, we feel a quietening within. This happens within our muscles, our minds, our breathing, and our heart rate. We feel that we have something we can do to get control back and decide how we are going to be thinking and feeling. This is the key.

All humans should practise breathing techniques. They are equivalent to putting fuel in a car if you want to go anywhere. Taking a moment to do some breathing and regular formal mindfulness practice is like fuelling ourselves up. It seems crazy to me that this is not as standard a daily practice as sleeping, eating, hydrating, cleaning our teeth and showering. This is why the majority of the world is running around on empty. We are not taking a moment out to refuel, get our baseline back and recharge our minds and bodies.

QUIETENING YOUR HEADSPACE TECHNIQUE

This quietening your headspace technique is the main formal mindfulness technique. Mindfulness is about creating a window of peace and stillness in the midst of the activity of life. We can learn to maintain our mental stability through the momentum of regular practice. This creates resilience in dealing with life's challenges such as stress, fast pace, turmoil, confusion, procrastination and decision making.

This technique involves you taking two to ten minutes out, twice a day, to quieten your thoughts. Find a quiet space. I would suggest sitting, not lying down, as this is not to relax you to sleep; this is actually a process of practising self-discipline and paying attention. You could be sitting in your car (pulled over of course), on a chair, or sitting up in bed. Get an alarm and set it for two minutes (the first time you practise this, two minutes will be enough. Later, as you'll see, you can build up to ten minutes).

Then your task is to sit there and focus and notice your breathing. Your breath is used as an anchor to the present moment. Your mind will not want to do this. Your mind will continue to throw thoughts at you; you will notice noises, feelings and thoughts of frustration; your mind will brainstorm ideas and sensations. These thoughts are like lost sheep: you need to herd them back to the breath.

So, as you are sitting there, noticing your breath, a thought comes. Notice it, but do not engage and have a conversation with it; instead, bring your concentration back to your breath. When a thought comes, do not block it; acknowledge it but do not follow its line of conversation or contemplation. Come back to the breath.

This sounds easy. It is not easy. It takes self-discipline to stay on task. Over time this can become a gentle and effortless exercise. You will become skilled in monitoring your mind closely, and each time your mind wanders you will simply came back to the breath. This rhythm of thinking is really like a flower if you map it out.

You have a distracted thought, you grab it and bring your concentration back to the breath.

Your breath

another thought

another thought to return to breath

another thought

another thought

Thoughts continue to come, and we keep herding our attention and refocusing back to our breath, but there are a lot of thoughts. By the end of our time it might look a little like this:

This is hard work and needs a lot of self-direction and self-discipline. We have a lot of traffic in the mind, which means a lot of herding our mind back to our breath. This is normal. Many clients have said to me that their mind just keeps wandering off. They think they are doing something wrong or it is not working. Actually, this is exactly what is supposed to happen, and it is the whole point. It is this process – of noticing our thoughts, and choosing not to engage in them, but instead to bring our concentration back to our breath – that is the actual mindfulness technique. It is about becoming in control of our thinking. Becoming mindful, and choosing which thoughts to engage in.

What if we have a thought and engage in it, get lost in it and completely forget about our breathing? That would look like this:

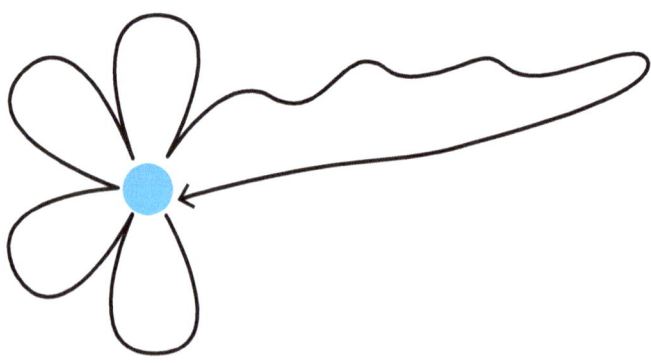

It is okay if you get lost in a thought for a while. We all do, to a degree, until we master this skill. When you realise that you have engaged in another thought, no problem; just bring your attention back to the breath and keep going. Our minds are going to start off pretty chaotic and messy until we practise this routinely and start to reap the benefits.

We start with:

Day 1:	2 minutes twice a day
Day 4:	4 minutes twice a day
Day 6:	6 minutes twice a day
Day 8:	8 minutes twice a day
Day 10:	10 minutes twice a day

By day ten, we have worked to your end goal of ten minutes twice a day.

The type of breathing that you do is really up to you. Some people really enjoy the structure of the inhale and then exhale to the count of seven; they find the structure helps them to stay disciplined in the herding of their thoughts. Others just focus on their breath, and notice their breath, in and out. Experiment and see what you prefer. There is no right or wrong. The key is the one focused concentration point of your breath. The breath has the added bonus of releasing physiological stress and helping us settle further into our parasympathetic nervous system.

This technique is profoundly beneficial for people suffering from anxiety or depression. There is pretty exciting research that finds significant reductions in anxiety and depressive mood when regular mindfulness practice is engaged in. With consistent practice, the anxious and depressive person finds their thoughts slow down dramatically, giving them not only a desperately wanted calming of the mind, but also less traffic to deal with, meaning fewer anxious or depressive thoughts to wrestle with.

HOT TIPS: HELP WITH MINDFULNESS PRACTICE; IT IS CHALLENGING

Your mind will wander off

We are now going to have a look at what happens in your mind while you are learning and practising formal mindfulness techniques. It is hard to do at first. Your mind will continue to wander off. It is like wrestling an octopus or trying to herd jelly. We can be everywhere and nowhere in our minds. It is essential to know that this is normal. You are not doing anything wrong.

Many people mistakenly think that a 'good meditation' is having little to no thinking. It is the opposite; a good meditation is about having a good session of redirecting your thoughts. The thoughts *will* come. That's normal and okay; it is what you *do* with them that makes it a good meditation. It is very hard to discipline the mind to refocus from our distractions and to maintain our concentration on just one thing, our breath. Hundreds, perhaps thousands, of people in session have told me, 'I'm not good at it, it's not working', or 'I can't do this', when their experience is normal. It is in fact the whole point. We start with a wandering, undisciplined mind, and gently, gently over time, we train the mind to focus. We train ourselves to be in charge of what we are concentrating on. If our attention moves away from the breath a hundred times, then we just return our focus to our breath a hundred times. In fact, you are being mindful in knowing that you are struggling. If you were not mindful, you would not have noticed your mind wandering off. The moment that you realise you are not present, you have actually become present.

So please take comfort. It is hard to do at the beginning, especially when you are extending the time out to ten minutes. It actually reminds me of running. I run regularly now, but before this became normal to me, I felt exhausted and very unsure I would ever feel comfortable running, let alone running a longer distance. But after persevering, little by little, the fitness improves, and we can run the distance comfortably. So we are becoming mindfully fit, and it is okay to start off unfit. This is the point!

Becoming mindfully fit: don't engage
We don't need to do anything with our thoughts, just catch them and then redirect our attention back to our breath. We are having time out from our thoughts, but we are not blocking them, or denying them. We are not stopping them or pushing them away. Trying to suppress our thoughts will only create greater tension and frustration, rather than mindful calmness.

We have a rare window to just be ourselves, and not to have to respond or do anything. Let things be as they are. Let your thoughts, emotions and sensations just be as they are. This includes being determined to just observe and accept your agitated emotions and physical discomfort in that moment. Do nothing about them; just allow them to *be*. This can be scary to do, but it is an extraordinary thing to experience and realise that not engaging in your thoughts can actually help overcome them. We don't engage therefore we don't fuel these painful experiences.

Don't judge, just observe

Just like we people-watch, this is 'thought watching'. In the previous section I advised you that you have the option not to *engage* in your thoughts; now I'm asking you also not to *judge* them. Just *watch* what is going on in your mind. We call this ability to observe your thoughts and not judge them being **nonjudgementally present**. Don't label your thoughts, sensations or feelings as right or wrong, good or bad; simply observe them. Be impartial, just a witness to the stream of thoughts that go through your mind.

Sometimes we will feel guilty for taking these minutes out for ourselves (which is ridiculous of course), and we think of all the things we 'should' be doing. This is especially important because if you do not herd this thought back to your breath and you engage in it, you might find that you jump up and impulsively get back into your daily obligations, cancelling your crucial mindfulness practice. Often our thoughts involve us judging ourselves. Or we just think *This is boring*. These are just more thoughts to observe. Observe your brain wanting to judge yourself in that moment. When this happens, grab the thought and herd it back to your breath.

Or your mind might ask you a question. Don't answer it; just return your concentration back to the breath.

A wonderful benefit from this mindfulness practice is that you get to observe all of the thoughts that try to hijack your concentration. You may discover that you are filled with worry, self-judgement, sadness, confusion, and anger. When you identify the themes of your thinking and feeling, you then have that information to work with. You also might discover that your body is feeling a lot of stress that you have just become used to. Your jaw might be clenched, your shoulders tensed up, or you might feel pain in your stomach. This awareness allows you to directly see your mind-body connection. You are witnessing how your thoughts and emotions are being expressed in your body.

You are strengthening your mindfulness skill, thought by thought
The exciting thing is that each time we notice a thought, grab it and then herd it back to focusing on our breath, we are strengthening our mindfulness. Think of them as 'reps' that build our mindfulness muscle. Each returning to our breath increases our control of our consciousness. It's very exciting and very rewarding.

You are actively cultivating your mindfulness skill. You are learning that thoughts, feelings and sensations are just thoughts, feelings and sensations. They are passing states that come and go, and you can choose not to be drawn into them. You can choose to not invest power into them that they do not have. You do not lose yourself to them. They do not define who you are; you are not a slave to them and you can be the master of them. You can learn to become detached from them with curious observation, then you can choose how to respond and manage them. You are taking back the power from the mental mutiny!

Do nothing
Here is a strange thought for our Western world: formal mindfulness involves not trying to get anywhere other than where you already are. This is a practice of non-doing. We are not doing, planning, grasping, changing, fixing, reacting, or moving in response to our thoughts. We are concentrating on our breath and herding our thoughts back. That's it. How peculiar to get off the Ferris wheel of life for ten minutes.

Finding time and sticking at it
It is essential to nourish, support, and strengthen your practice. Theories mean nothing if we don't practise them. How do we remember? How do we stick at it and not forget to prioritise ten minutes of formal mindfulness practice twice a day?

The answer is that first we need to recognise that we *want* the benefits of formal mindfulness; we want a calm mind, we want enhanced mental health. Second, we make it routine, so that it is a no-brainer. It is not whether we will do it, it is 'just what we do'. We remember to clean our teeth, have a shower, put our clothes in (or towards!) the dirty clothes basket, drink our morning coffee, put our car keys in their spot at home, hang our towels up, wear underwear and clothing – all these things because 1) we value them, and 2) it is our routine. So too with mindfulness practice. It just needs to become part of our lifestyle because we value creating and maintaining a calm mind. It is not an initial burst of enthusiasm and novelty; it is part of our routine lifestyle. A strong commitment is needed.

The first ten-minute practice could be scheduled in your morning routine, and the second ten-minute practice in your afternoon/evening routine. I personally do my morning practice ten minutes after my morning coffee, sitting in bed. I can usually manage it without one of our kids running in. If I'm disturbed, that's okay; we do what we can. You definitely cannot become agitated and intense about this practice – otherwise you are missing the point. While it is serious in its benefits, and we need to prioritise making the time, we need to be light in its actual doing. So, kid interruptions happen. That's okay. My afternoon ten minutes can be when I am doing school pick up and I am waiting in my parked car, or after I have got the kids to bed.

Jon, my husband, is very consistent with his formal mindfulness practice. Between us, our code is 'ten minutes'. It is definitely a bonus (but in no way essential) when both partners practice formal mindfulness, because there is a mutual valuing of taking the time. I had one client who would take her ten minutes during her lunch break; it was her lunch-time ritual. To do this, she decided to go to a toilet cubicle at her work. This was the only place where she could cocoon herself from the world at work. Hey, whatever works! Top points for creativity! I personally have been doing this technique for fifteen years, and I am rewarded with fairly quiet traffic in my mind, both during my day and during my mindfulness sessions. People around me may be physically buff, but perhaps I am mentally buff? It's an amusing thought.

> An ounce of practice is better than tons of theory.

We are in very real danger of being swept up in the swirling fog of life. We can lose our bearings when we get caught up in the high pace of life; confusion, anxiety and depression can take us away from our previous advances in self-awareness and our regular practice of formal mindfulness. We get caught up in the mouse wheel and don't even know it. But think of it this way: if you are going to be using your car for a lot of driving at a hectic, non-stop and pressured pace, then isn't it that much more important to put fuel in the car? Wouldn't it be a crazy notion to be too busy to put fuel in the car, but expect to drive far and hard? What would end up happening? The car would stop. So too with us. When we push hard and get lost in our mental spirals of agitation, we do not fuel up, and then – surprise, surprise – we end up in an anxious or depressive heap. So, let's keep the 'fuel the car' analogy, and remember to fuel up with our formal mindfulness practice. It is just being really smart and strategic in life.

> Regular practice and self-discipline are essential to harnessing the power of mindfulness.

CHAPTER 40
NEUROPLASTICITY

There is ground-breaking research coming out about the remarkable capacity of the brain to reorganise itself and adapt to various sensory experiences. We know that the human brain continues to change in its actual structure in response to repetitive experiences over time. It is not a rigid form. The brain is malleable. This means we can actually change, reshape and rewire the structure of the brain (and therefore the function of our brain) based on behaviours that we repeatedly do. This is a **plasticity** in the brain.

This means that what we call to our minds actually shapes our brain – and this is from not just our childhood but all across our lifespan. This is good and bad news. Trauma can be a repetitive experience (in that we continue to think about it after it happens) that can lead to negative changes in the brain. The good news is that repetitive, positive, healing experiences can be restorative to the brain. Positive, corrective experiences are therapeutic and create this recovery. Laboratory research has found that repetitive meditative practices create positive neuroplastic changes in the brain. These changes to the structure of the brain reflect mental well-being. This in turn helps protect and buffer us from future stressful and traumatic experiences.

The mind can change the brain.

CHAPTER 41
SELF-HYPNOSIS

As a quick note, we can also learn the related skill of self-hypnosis. It is different to formal mindfulness practice, however, as we are not tapping into our awareness of our moment, but rather taking ourselves *away* from our moment into an alternate focal point and going deeper into a subconscious state. I won't cover it here, but it is an extraordinary skill, experience and strength to have. I have used self-hypnosis during childbirth. The midwives couldn't believe that I was so advanced in labour because of my calm physical state. The skill of self-hypnosis is remarkable and astonishing in allowing us to block our processing and therefore block the experience of physical and psychological pain.

IN CONCLUSION: KNOW THYSELF

The goal is for us to optimally skill up to reduce our psychological and emotional pain and turmoil, and increase our meaning in life – and, by doing so, increase our happiness. The benefits from this skill set are immediate and just keep growing and growing. This is about accepting the uncertainty, fallibility and imperfection that makes us human, and finding ways to be happy in our imperfect world. Working towards mastering our thoughts, negotiating our emotions and soothing our reactive nervous system is the key to our ability to live well. When we get in the driver's seat, hands on the steering wheel, we can confidently approach the unknowns and inevitable challenges in life. We can actively nagivate our human experience.

FURTHER READING

The following books contain a great deal of wisdom and insight that show us how we can come through unimaginable trauma and still live meaningfully.

Albom, M (1988), *Tuesdays with Morrie*, Hodder, Sydney.

Frankl, VE (1984), *Man's search for meaning: an introduction to logotherapy*, Simon & Schuster, New York.

O'Donohue, J (1997), *Anam Cara: a book of Celtic wisdom*, Harper Perennial, New York.

And, finally, if you wish to explore the topics I have touched on briefly in this book more deeply, you might like to try the other books in the 'Signposts for Living' series by Dr Kirsten Hunter:

Book 2: Understanding Myself – Be an Expert

Book 3: Mindfulness and State of Flow – Living with Purpose and Passion

Book 4: Understanding Others – Loved Ones to Tricky Ones

Book 5: Parenting – Love, Pride, Apprenticeship

Book 6: Nailing Being an Adult – Have the Skills

ACKNOWLEDGEMENTS

To Jon, my beautiful husband, your support is constant. I can always rely on you to be in my corner, patiently championing me on while I sit typing away. With writing, having someone who believes in you makes all the difference. Thank you that it is always 'us' facing the next challenge, the next hurdle. I love you.

My devoted mum has been the rock through my childhood and every chapter of my adulthood. No child could have a more extraordinary mum. I'm proud of you and I love you.

Our five boys, Lachlan, James, Tobias, Jack, and George, when you heard that your mum was writing books, non-fiction and fiction, your response was simply 'of course she is'. When you heard mum was publishing, your response was 'of course she is'. When we talk about the book being successful in reaching a wide audience, your response, 'of course it will'. You boys are so beautiful. Ever-resounding support, thank you. I love you.

Vanya Lowther, you are the smartest person I know, and perhaps the wisest. You are also my closest and my lifelong friend. Thank you for taking on the mammoth task of being the first person to put your eyes on the *Signposts for Living* books. Your perseverance, your contribution and brainpower was and is so appreciated. I love you.

Jane Smith, I agree with Stephen King, 'to write is human, to edit is divine'. Thank you for your eye for detail, your grammatical wizardry and staying fresh when there was so much work to do. You're a talented gem.

ABOUT THE AUTHOR

Dr Kirsten Hunter is a clinical psychologist with 20 years' experience working with children, adolescents, adults, and couples across the expanse of clinical areas. Between running her private practice, enjoying time with her family, and writing her books, Kirsten juggles a range of passions – particularly for scuba diving and hiking. Kirsten is known for diving deep into life, creating and embracing all of life's opportunities. Born in Brisbane, she now lives in Toowoomba, Australia, with her six men: her husband and their five sons. Even their pets are male ...

www.ingramcontent.com/pod-product-compliance
Lightning Source LLC
Chambersburg PA
CBHW041957080526
44588CB00021B/2771